LANGUAGE BUILDER

In Sync 3

Lindsay White
Liz Kilbey
Ingrid Freebairn
Jonathan Bygrave
Judy Copage

Welcome to the **Language Builder!**

This **Language Builder** will give you more practice in the grammar, vocabulary, functions, and skills that are in your Student Book. The Language Builder is divided into two parts: a Workbook and a Grammar Bank.

Workbook

The first part of the Language Builder is the **Workbook**. This contains practice exercises for the grammar, vocabulary, functions, and skills in your Student Book. Most of the exercises in the Workbook lessons are at two levels of difficulty: easier (★) and more difficult (★★). There are also *Consolidation* exercises, which provide practice of several language points. In addition, there is an *Extra challenge!* exercise (★★★) in each unit, which gives you the opportunity to do a more challenging activity.

Grammar Bank

The second part of the Language Builder is the **Grammar Bank**. This contains *Grammar Summary* pages with examples and notes to help you remember grammar rules. These are followed by *Grammar Practice* exercises. You can do these exercises as a follow-up to the exercises in the Workbook, or you can use them later to help you review.

We hope that this Language Builder will help you in your English studies.

Have fun and stay *In Sync*!

Contents

She doesn't know many people.

Your life

1

Phrases

1 ★ Match the sentences (1–5) with the replies (a–e).

1 These are my sisters, Beth and Amy.

2 How's it going?

3 Do you want to meet my new friends?

4 What's he like?

5 Do you like Ian and Dan?

a) Don't worry, he isn't boring!

b) Good, thanks.

c) Nice to meet you.

d) Yes, I do. We hang out together on the weekends.

e) That would be great.

Vocabulary: Personality adjectives

2 ★ Choose the correct answer.

1 My best friend is great—he's always __b__ .

  a) stuck-up   b) cheerful   c) boring

2 Don't leave money on the table. Some people are ____ .

  a) impatient   b) relaxed   c) dishonest

3 I love babies. They are so ____ !

  a) cute   b) lazy   c) mean

4 My brother is ____ but he never gets good grades on tests.

  a) moody   b) intelligent   c) selfish

5 We enjoy parties because we're ____ .

  a) smart   b) serious   c) sociable

6 Don't say unkind things to my little sister— she's very ____ .

  a) talkative   b) sensitive   c) friendly

3 ★★ Complete the sentences with words from the box. There is one extra word.

> • confident • honest • impatient • modest • patient • ~~selfish~~ • serious

What's your best friend like?

George is always generous! He's never *selfish*.

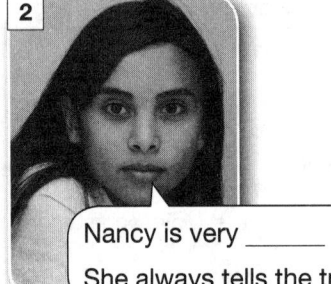

Nancy is very _____ . She always tells the truth.

Ryan doesn't do silly things. He's very _____ .

Lucy isn't stuck-up. She's always _____ .

Alex is _____ . He doesn't mind speaking in class.

Lily is usually cheerful, but she isn't ____ with small children.

Grammar: Simple present and present continuous

4 ★ Circle the correct answers.

1 She can't play soccer now. Her brother *helps* / (*is helping*) her with her homework.

2 I never sit with my best friend in class because he *talks* / *is talking* all the time.

3 Right now we *watch* / *are watching* our favorite TV show.

4 We *don't go* / *aren't going* to school on Saturday or Sunday.

5 I'm sorry, *I don't remember* / *I'm not remembering* your name.

5 ★★ Complete the e-mail with the correct form of the verbs in the box.

> • be • eat • learn • make • not like
> • not speak • play • understand • want
> • work • ~~write~~

From:	Leah
≡▾ To:	Alice

Hi Alice,

I ¹*'m writing* this e-mail on my friend Kate's computer. Right now, Kate ² _____ a snack for us. We always ³ _____ sandwiches with cheese. We always have fruit smoothies because we ⁴ _____ tea or coffee.

There is a new Spanish boy in our class so we ⁵ _____ lots of new vocabulary in our Spanish lessons. His name's Juan. His mom and dad ⁶ _____ here for a year. Juan ⁷ _____ English very well but he ⁸ _____ everything.

Juan and Theo (Kate's brother) ⁹ _____ friends. Right now, they ¹⁰ _____ tennis in the park.

I can hear Kate calling me—she ¹¹ _____ some help with the snack. Please write to me soon!

Lots of love,

Leah

Consolidation

6 Complete the conversation.

James: Hi, Ethan. **1** *How is school?* (how/be/school?)

Ethan: Good, thanks.

James: Are you in 10ᵗʰ grade now?

Ethan: **2** _____ (yes/I/be.)

James: **3** _____ (who/be/your French teacher?)

Ethan: It's the new teacher, Monsieur Brun.

James: **4** _____ (what/be/he/like?)

Ethan: He's great! **5** _____ _____ (he/speak French/all the time.) **6** _____ (I/like) his classes because **7** _____ (they/be) fun. This week **8** _____ (we/write) newspaper articles in French.

James: That sounds interesting. **9** _____ _____ (you/work/with a partner?)

Ethan: Yes, **10** _____ _____ (I/work/with a new student.) His name's Rob.

James: **11** _____ (I/know/him.) He hangs out with the soccer team.

Where are we going?

Grammar: *Wh-* and *How* questions (simple present and present continuous)

1 ★ Circle the correct question words.

1 *Who / Where / (Which)* movie do you want to see?

2 *Who / Where / Which* lives there?

3 *Where / Which / When* shoes do you like?

4 *Who / Where / What* are we?

5 It's Saturday! *Why / What / How* are you waking me up?

6 *When / How / What* do you have under your T-shirt, sir?

2 ★★ Complete the conversation with words and phrases from the box.

> • How much • Who's • What does • ~~How often~~
> • How long • What do

Sergio: **1** *How often* do you fly home to the U.K., Jenna?

Jenna: Not very often because it's a very long trip.

Sergio: **2** _____ is the flight?

Jenna: It's about ten hours.

Sergio: That's a long time! **3** _____ is a ticket?

Jenna: I don't know! My parents buy the tickets.

Sergio: **4** _____ you do for ten hours? Is it boring?

Jenna: No, I usually watch the "film."

Sergio: **5** _____ "film" mean?

Jenna: It means movie!

Sergio: I know, I'm joking! **6** _____ your favorite movie—*film*—star?

Jenna: I like Zac Efron.

3a ★★ Complete the questions with a word or phrase.

1 *How far* is it from Seattle to San Francisco?

2 _____ does the number 15 bus go?

3 _____ bus goes to Green Park?

4 _____ is the train late?

5 _____ has our tickets?

6 _____ people live in London?

b ★ Now match the answers (a–f) with the questions (1–6).

- [ ] a) About 7,500,000.
- [ ] b) I don't know. It doesn't always arrive on time.
- [ ] c) I have them! They're in my backpack.
- [ ] d) It goes to Downtown Seattle.
- [1] e) It's about 800 miles.
- [ ] f) The number 7 goes there.

4 ★★ Complete the questions. Use words from the box and the verbs in parentheses.

• what • where • ~~where~~ • which • who • why

Theo: Hi Mom!

Mom: Hi, Theo. 1 *Where are* (be) you?

Theo: We're at the bus station.

Mom: We? 2 _____ (be) you with?

Theo: Carlos.

Mom: 3 _____ (be) you at the bus station?

Theo: We're waiting for the bus!

Mom: 4 _____ (be) you _____ (go)?

Theo: We're going to a soccer game.

Mom: 5 _____ teams _____ (play)?

Theo: It's our school against Deacon High School.

Mom: 6 _____ time _____ the game _____ (end)?

Theo: I think it ends at six o'clock.

Mom: OK. See you later. Bye.

Use your English: Ask for help with words in English

5 ★ Complete the questions and answers.

1 **Q:** W*hat's* the w*ord* for "biscuit" in American English?

  A: It's "cookie."

2 **Q:** H_____ d_____ y_____ say "pavement" in American English?

  A: Y_____ s_____ "sidewalk."

3 **Q:** What's a "lift" called in the U.S.?

  A: It's _____ an "elevator."

6 ★★ Complete the text with American English.

Every year my family has a summer 1 _____ (holiday) in New York. My dad likes walking so we don't take the 2 _____ (underground) often. I want to take a yellow 3 _____ (taxi) but Dad says they are too expensive. We always stay at the Broadway Hotel—there are lots of stairs and there's no 4 _____ (lift)! We always see a 5 _____ (film) in Times Square.

Consolidation

7 Read the article and complete the interview.

ZAC EFRON

Full name: **Zachary David Alexander Efron**
Birthday: **10/18/1987**
Home: **California**
Pets: **two dogs (Puppy and Dreamer) and a cat (Simon)**
Right now: **relaxing between movies!**

Interviewer: 1 *What's your full name?*

  (what / full name?)

Zac: 2 *Zachary David Alexander Efron*

Interviewer: 3 _____

  (when / birthday?)

Zac: 4 _____

Interviewer: 5 _____

  (where / live?)

Zac: 6 _____

Interviewer: 7 _____

  (who / Simon? be / he / your best friend?)

Zac: 8 _____

Interviewer: 9 _____

  (how many / pets / you have?)

Zac: 10 _____

Interviewer: 11 _____

  (what / do / right now?)

Zac: I'm relaxing between movies.

While we were talking . . .

Vocabulary: Jobs

1 ★ **Circle the words that don't belong.**

1 actor	director	(teacher)
2 politician	model	hairdresser
3 police officer	firefighter	ski instructor
4 cab driver	reporter	journalist
5 chef	vet	waiter

2 ★★ **Who uses these things? Write the jobs.**

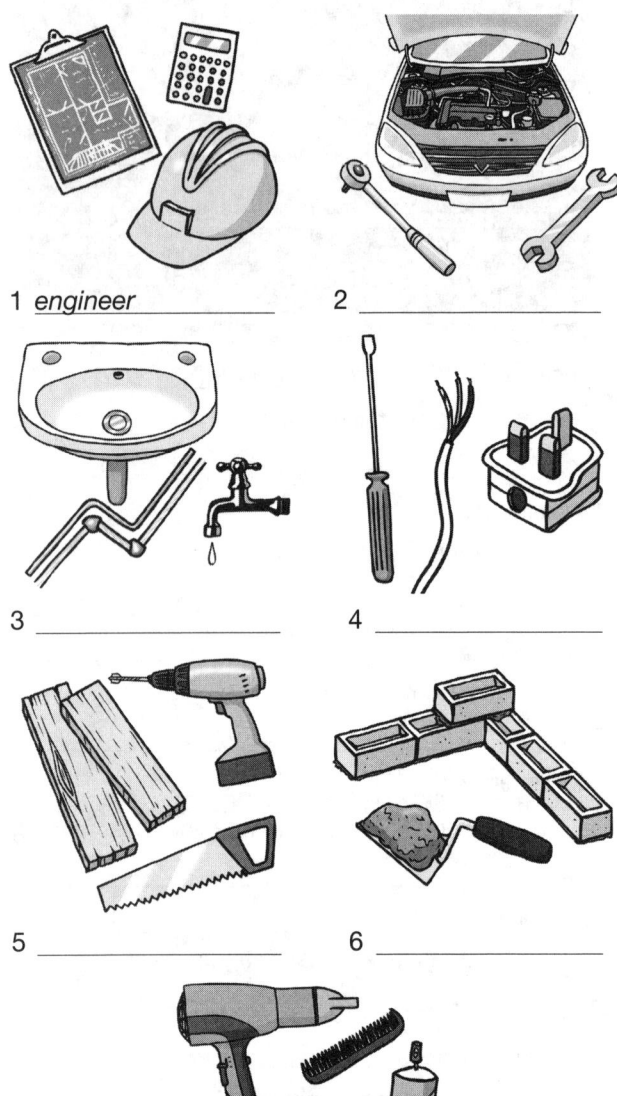

1 *engineer*

2 _____

3 _____

4 _____

5 _____

6 _____

7 _____

Grammar: Simple past and past continuous; Time markers: *when*, *while/as*

3 ★ **Complete the sentences with *when* or *while*.**

1 *While* we were waiting outside the movie theater, we saw our Science teacher.

2 I was standing in line for tickets _____ my phone rang.

3 _____ I was watching the movie, I ate a big bag of popcorn.

4 _____ the movie ended, everyone was crying.

4 ★★ **Complete the sentences with the correct form of the verbs in parentheses.**

1 While the vet *was looking* (look) at my cat, it *jumped* (jump) off the table.

2 As the actor _____ (leave) the theater, some fans _____ (take) photographs.

3 The robbers _____ (arrive) while the cashiers _____ (count) the money.

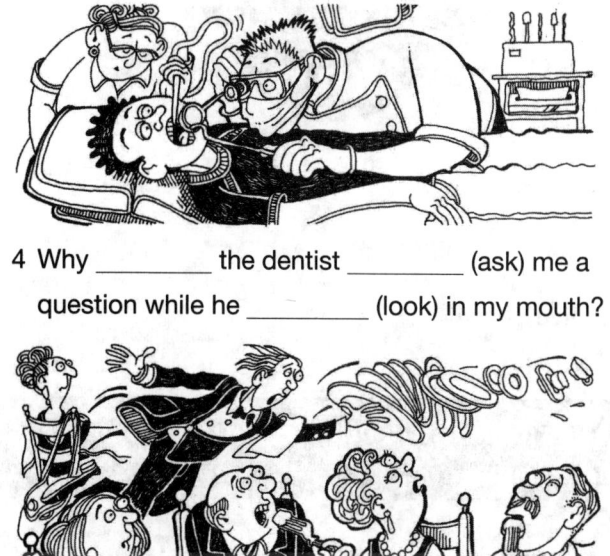

4 Why _____ the dentist _____ (ask) me a question while he _____ (look) in my mouth?

5 As the waiter _____ (carry) the plates to the table, he _____ (fall down).

Consolidation

5 Complete the text with the correct form of the verbs in the box.

> • arrive • ask • eat • fly • know • ~~look~~ • see
> • show • sit • talk • visit • wait

How Louis and Max became movie stars

Last year two schoolboys' dreams came true when they acted in the new movie *Dance School*.

While the director of *Dance School* **1** *was looking* for young actors to be students in her next movie, she **2** _____ lots of schools in Los Angeles and other U.S. towns and cities. She **3** _____ hundreds of teenagers but she didn't like any of

them! When she **4** _____ home to Los Angeles from Dallas, she **5** _____ next to a journalist on the plane. As they **6** _____ lunch, they **7** _____ about their families. The journalist **8** _____ the director a photograph of his two teenage sons. When the director looked at the photograph, she **9** _____ the boys were perfect for her movie. When the plane **10** _____ in Los Angeles, the boys, Louis and Max, **11** _____ for their father. The director **12** _____ them to be in the next *Dance School* movie. Their answer? A very loud, "Yes!"

Extra challenge

6 ★★★ Answer the journalist's questions.

Journalist: Can I ask you some questions for my magazine?

You: *Yes, you can.*

Journalist: What's your name?

You: _____

Journalist: Were you born in this town?

You: _____

Journalist: Who do you live with?

You: _____

Journalist: I want to ask about your friends. What kind of people do you like?

You: _____

Journalist: Did you have the same friends in elementary school?

You: _____

Journalist: How often do you see your friends?

You: _____

Journalist: What were you and your friends doing at four o'clock last Saturday afternoon?

You: _____

Journalist: One more question. Which book are you reading right now?

You: _____

A multicultural society

Read

1 ★ Read the texts. Where do Jina, Tom, and Morgan live?

Jina: _____   Tom: _____   Morgan: _____

> According to recent estimates, about 6.6 million Americans live in other countries. Some popular places are Korea, Mexico, Costa Rica, and Europe.

Jina
My dad's parents moved from Chicago to Korea in the 1960s. My grandfather is an engineer and he got a job in Seoul. My dad was born a few months after they arrived. My mom's family is Korean, so she was born there. Mom, Dad, and I all speak Korean, but I'm learning English so I can talk to my dad's family. My grandfather has an American accent and my grandmother still speaks English most of the time!

Tom
I live in Mexico with my parents and older sister. My mom is Mexican and my dad is American. They met while my mom was studying veterinary science in the U.S. They moved to Puebla when they got married because Mom wanted to be near her family. We speak Spanish and English and we celebrate all the Mexican holidays, like Cinco be Mayo, Mexican Independence Day, and Día de los Muertos.

Morgan
My parents came to Brazil to study the plants in the rain forest. They're scientists and they met in graduate school. They moved here in 1990. I was born in the U.S. so I have a U.S. passport, but Brazil is my home. My Portuguese is better than my English! My dad's parents visited in 2002 and they loved it. While they were visiting, they decided to retire here! Now they live about five miles away from us.

New words

2 ★★ Match the new words (1–6) with the definitions (a–f).

1 Korean
2 accent
3 veterinary science
4 independence
5 retire

a) (noun) the medical care of sick animals
b) (noun) the state of being free from the control of another country
c) (noun) a way of speaking that shows that a person comes from a particular place
d) (verb) to stop work because of old age or illness
e) (adjective) relating to Korea and its people

Comprehension

3 ★★ In your notebook, answer each question about Jina, Tom, and Morgan.

1 When did their families move to another country?

2 Why did their families move there?

3 Which languages do they speak?

Listen

4 ★ (2) Listen to Caitlin interviewing Liam, a new boy in her class. Complete the sentences with either *Ireland* or *the U.S.*

1 Liam lives in _____ now.

2 Liam's grandparents traveled from _____ to _____ .

3 Liam's parents were born in _____ .

5 ★★ Listen again. Copy the ideas map in your notebook and complete it with information about Liam.

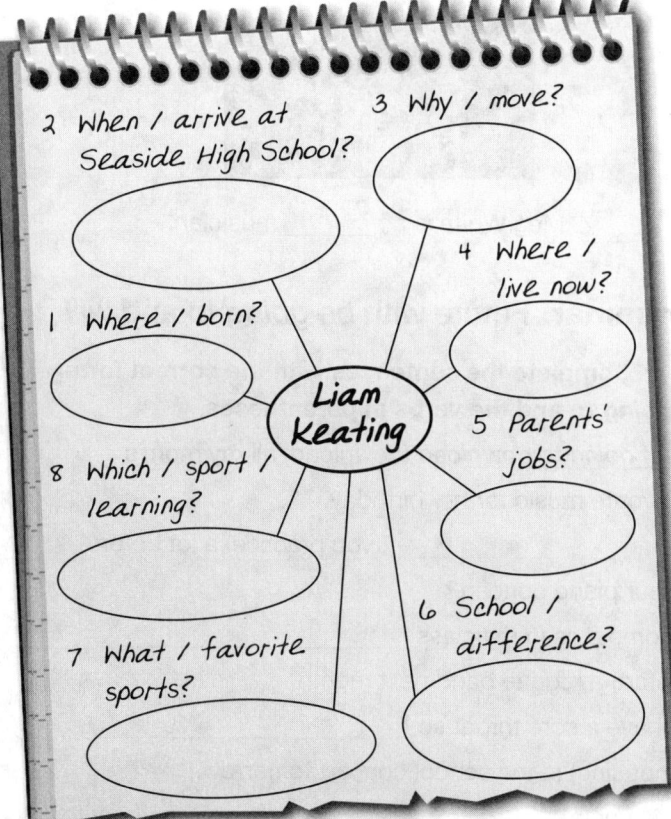

Write

Learning strategy: Making an ideas map
Remember! An ideas map can help you to organize and plan your writing.

6 ★ Use the notes to complete the text.

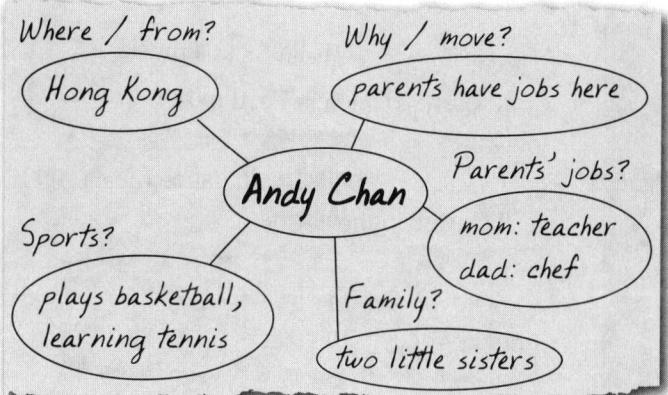

Where / from? — Hong Kong
Why / move? — parents have jobs here
Parents' jobs? — mom: teacher, dad: chef
Sports? — plays basketball, learning tennis
Family? — two little sisters

Andy Chan

http://www.seaside_school.new_students.edu

Who's new?

Welcome to Andy Chan!

Andy started at our school four weeks ago. ¹*He is from Hong Kong* . The Chan family moved here because ² _____ . Andy's mom ³ _____ and ⁴ _____ . Andy ⁵ _____ : Ming is nine and San is five. Andy likes sports. He ⁶ _____ and he ⁷ _____ .

7 ★★ Read about another new student. On a piece of paper, write an article for the school website.

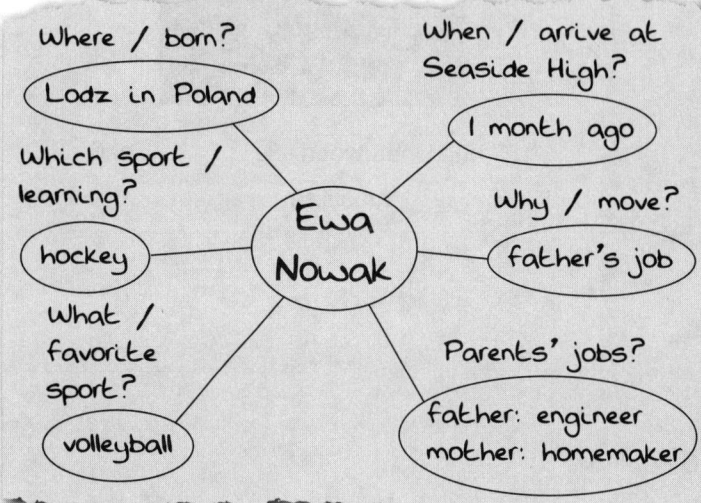

Where / born? — Lodz in Poland
Which sport / learning? — hockey
What / favorite sport? — volleyball
When / arrive at Seaside High? — 1 month ago
Why / move? — father's job
Parents' jobs? — father: engineer, mother: homemaker

Ewa Nowak

Music and movies

2

Vocabulary: Types of music

1 ★★ Complete the words to make types of music.

1. Joan Baez, the queen of f<u>olk</u> music, is going to perform in Portland on May 23.

2. T_____ is electronic dance music. It started in the 1980s.

3. Christina Aguilera's fans will love her new p_____ single.

4. I don't usually like r___p but Jay Z's *The Blueprint3* is excellent.

5. "Respect" by s_____ singer Aretha Franklin is a fantastic song.

6. Dear Clare, My parents won't let me play h_____-h_____ music in the house.

2 ★★ Complete the information.

1. Carrie Underwood is a c_____ and w_____ musician.

2. Jamie Cullum is a j_____ musician.

3. Kyung Wha Chung is a c_____l musician.

4. Meg White is a r_____ musician.

Grammar: Future with *be going to* and *will*

3 ★ Complete the sentences with the correct form of *going to* and the verbs in parentheses.

1. I*'m going to download* (download) all my mom's favorite music for her birthday.

2. _____ (you practice) a lot before your piano concert?

3. Some girls in my class _____ (start) a reggae band next month.

4. I have a sore throat so I _____ (not sing) in the school concert tomorrow.

5. My uncle _____ (teach) me how to play the guitar.

4 ★★ Complete the conversation with *will* and verbs from the box. There is one extra verb.

- be • download • get • listen • not be
- ~~not buy~~ • not have • pay • play

Sally: People probably **1** *won't buy* music in the future. I think the music companies
2 _____ money from advertising on the Internet and the music **3** _____ free.

Henry: I don't agree with you. I think we **4** _____ for music but it **5** _____ expensive.

Sally: Why will it be cheap?

Henry: Because millions of people **6** _____ their music from the Internet. A few older people **7** _____ to CDs but most people **8** _____ CD players.

5 ★★ Complete the sentences with the correct form of *will* or *going to* and the verbs in parentheses.

1 Let's go. I think you*'ll love* (love) it.

2 I _____ (hate) this!

3 I _____ (take) keyboard lessons! I _____ (be) great!

4 He _____ (not be) a good keyboard player.

5 I think they _____ (start) a band when they are teenagers!

6 Oh no! They _____ (start) a band.

Consolidation

6 Complete the conversations with the correct form of *will* or *be going to*.

Dan: **1** *Are you going to* go to the show next weekend?

Tom: I don't know. How much are the tickets?

Dan: I **2** _____ check the website tonight. I **3** _____ tell you tomorrow.

Tom: Thanks. Do you know who is **4** _____ play this year?

Dan: I can't remember all the names but I know lots of good bands **5** _____ be there.

Tom: I **6** _____ ask my parents if I can go.

Dan: I'm sure they **7** _____ say "no."

The next day

Dan: Hi Tom. The tickets are $20.

Tom: That's not bad!

Dan: I **8** _____ buy my ticket online. Do you want me to get yours?

Tom: Yes, please. Actually, I think I **9** _____ take my sister for her birthday. Can you get me two tickets, please?

Dan: Sure, no problem.

Tom: How **10** _____ get there?

Dan: I **11** _____ take the monorail with my older brother.

Tom: Great! We **12** _____ do that, too.

Phrases

1a ★ Complete the phrases.

1 Wh _ _ 's _ p?

2 ch _ _ k it out

3 not m _ _ h

b ★★ Now complete the conversations with the phrases.

1 Carlos: Hey, Pete. _____?

   Pete: Julia and I are going to watch the Seattle Sounders game at Tina's house. Do you want to come?

2 Alain: What are you doing on Sunday?

   Jess: _____ . Why?

3 Hannah: Zoe and I are going to the new restaurant in town on Saturday. Would you like to come with us?

   Jane: I'm busy on Saturday. You two can _____ and tell me about it.

Grammar: Present continuous form for future fixed arrangements

2 ★★ Complete the sentences with the present continuous form of the verbs in parentheses.

1 I*'m visiting* (visit) my grandparents next Saturday.

2 _____ (Jane come) to your party?

3 We _____ (go) ice-skating on Friday night. Would you like to come?

4 _____ (Sarah and Max do) anything this weekend?

5 We _____ (not go) on vacation this summer.

6 Leo _____ (not play) with the band on Saturday.

7 I _____ (not eat) in that café again. The food's terrible!

3 ★★ Complete the conversation with the present continuous form of the verbs in the box.

> • clean • do • drive • get • go • leave
> • not do • practice • sleep • stay

Poppy: What **1** *are* you *doing* this weekend?

Harry: I **2** _____ to a wedding on Saturday. My cousin Suzy and her boyfriend Steve **3** _____ married.

Poppy: Where's the wedding?

Harry: It's in Spokane. My uncle **4** _____ us all there in his car. It's a long way from Seattle to Spokane so we **5** _____ on Friday night.

Poppy: **6** _____ you _____ with relatives in Spokane?

Harry: Yes, we are. We're all staying at my aunt's house. My cousins have a tent so all the teenagers **7** _____ in the yard! What are you doing this weekend?

Poppy: I **8** _____ much. On Saturday I **9** _____ my bedroom. On Sunday I **10** _____ my clarinet for the school concert.

Use your English: Make arrangements

4 ★ Number the sentences in the correct order.

Conversation 1

☐ a) *Fright Night*. It's a horror movie.

☐ b) We're going to the 6:30 show.

☐ c) What are you seeing?

☐ d) What time are you going?

[1] e) Would you like to go to the movies with us tomorrow?

☐ f) OK, that sounds great. I'll see you there.

Conversation 2

- [ ] a) When are you meeting them?
- [ ] b) I'm meeting Jack and his sister for pizza this weekend. Do you want to come with me?
- [ ] c) I'm afraid I can't. I'm working on Saturday.
- [ ] d) At lunchtime on Saturday.
- [ ] e) Another time!

Consolidation

5 Use the information in Jo's diary to complete the conversation.

Monday	have dinner with grandparents
Tuesday	play trumpet in school concert
Wednesday	go to the movies with Emily
Thursday	meet Danny in town
Friday	paintballing!
Saturday	play soccer, go to rock concert
Sunday	do my homework!

Emily: Do you want to go for a bike ride on Tuesday?

Jo: Sorry, I can't. I **1** _'m playing the trumpet in the school concert_ .

Emily: Are you doing anything on Monday?

Jo: Yes, I **2** _____ .

Emily: I'm seeing you on Wednesday.

Jo: Yes, we **3** _____ .

Emily: **4** _____ you _____ on Saturday?

Jo: No, I **5** _____ . I **6** _____ . Would you like to go?

Emily: I'm afraid I can't. I'm doing my homework because I'm going to a jazz festival on Sunday.

Jo: Oh, well. I **7** _____ on Sunday!

Extra challenge!

6 ★★★ Complete the conversation with *will*, *going to,* or the present continuous form of the verbs in the box.

- ask (×2) • buy • come • ~~do~~ • not do
- see (×2) • watch (×2)

Mark: What **1** _are_ you _doing_ tonight, Oliver?

Oliver: Not much. Why?

Mark: I **2** _____ anything either. Do you want to watch a movie?

Oliver: Yes, that sounds great.

Mark: OK, we **3** _____ what's on the movie channel. There are always lots of choices.

Oliver: I **4** _____ Mom for some soda and popcorn.

Mark: Good idea. See you later.

Five minutes later

Maria: Hi, Oliver, what are you doing tonight?

Oliver: Mark and I **5** _____ a movie at his house. Would you like to come, too?

Maria: What **6** _____ you _____ ?

Oliver: I don't know. We **7** _____ what's on.

Maria: Thanks—I **8** _____ .
I **9** _____ some snacks.

Oliver: Don't worry—I **10** _____ my mom for some soda and popcorn.

Maria: A movie, soda, and popcorn! It sounds great!

It was much more exciting than . . .

Vocabulary: Adjectives of opinion

1 ★ Write the adjectives in the chart.

- ~~amazing~~ • ~~awful~~ • boring • dull
- excellent • fabulous • fantastic
- fascinating • lousy • terrible

Positive meaning	Negative meaning
amazing	*awful*

2 ★★ Complete the sentences with adjectives from the box. There are two extra adjectives.

- ~~awesome~~ • boring • confusing • cool
- excellent • funny • sad • scary

Did you enjoy the movie?

1 Yes! It was _awesome_ !

2 Yes, we did. We laughed a lot— it was very _____ .

3 Yes, it was _____ . We liked it a lot.

4 Yes, it was _____ . I cried for an hour!

5 I don't know. I was asleep. It was very _____ .

6 The children hated it. It was _____ .

Grammar: Comparison of adjectives

3 ★ Put the words in order to make sentences about the actors.

1 is than funnier the Rob others .

Rob _is funnier than the others._

2 actor is the a than worse others Al .

Al _____

3 than is Jim cheerful less Rob .

Jim _____

4 as isn't funny Jim and Rob Al as .

Al _____

5 than is better much Al Jim .

Jim _____

4 ★★ **Read the information. Then complete the text with comparative or superlative forms of the adjectives in parentheses.**

Reese Witherspoon
Born: 1976
$15–20 million for each movie

Renée Zellweger
Born: 1969
$10–15 million for each movie

Halle Berry
Born: 1966
$10 million for each movie

Reese Witherspoon, Renée Zellweger, and Halle Berry are three top Hollywood actresses. Reese Witherspoon is **1** _the youngest_ (young) and she is also **2** _____ (expensive). She gets more than $15 million for each movie.

Halle Berry is **3** _____ (old) the other two but she is **4** _____ (not expensive) the other two actors. She "only" gets about $10 million per movie!

Renée Zellweger is **5** _____ (young) Halle Berry but **6** _____ (old) Reese Witherspoon. She is **7** _____ (expensive) Halle Berry but **8** _____ (expensive) Reese Witherspoon.

Which one is the best actress? Some people think Renée is **9** _____ (good) the other two. Other people think Reese is **10** _____ (good) Renée. Some people say Halle Berry is **11** _____ _____ (not good) the others but she has lots of fans. She definitely isn't **12** _____ (bad) actor in Hollywood!

Consolidation

5 Choose the correct answers.

> I love the three *Bourne* movies: they are **1** _b_ ! They are **2** ____ the *James Bond* movies. The *Bourne* movies are all **3** ____ but the first one, *The Bourne Identity*, is **4** ____ . I watched *The Bourne Ultimatum* with my dad and he said it was **5** ____ movie in the world. He didn't understand it! (I disagree. I think *The Matrix* is **6** ____ *The Bourne Ultimatum*.)

> The action in all three movies is **7** ____ . There is never a **8** ____ moment.

1 a) dull   b) fantastic   c) terrible
2 a) the best   b) better   c) as good as
3 a) excellent   b) sad   c) boring
4 a) the more exciting than
   b) the most exciting than   c) the most exciting
5 a) the most confusing   b) more confusing
   c) more confusing than
6 a) much more confusing than
   b) n't as confusing as   c) less confusing than
7 a) awful   b) awesome   c) funny
8 a) dull   b) exciting   c) scary

INTEGRATED
CONSOLIDATION
SKILLS

Music to change the world

Learning strategy: Previewing
Remember! Before you read, look at the title, pictures, and headings.

Read

1 ★ Look at the title of the text and the photo. What do you think the text will be about?

2 ★ Read and check your answer.

Music to make you better

We know about famous people raising money for charity, but what about all the work done by unknown people? Ben Winterburn is a young man from Leeds in northern England. When he was eighteen, he was very sick and spent a lot of time in the hospital.

When he got better, he decided he wanted to help other sick teenagers. He loves music, so he organized a charity concert. He arranged the groups, the venue, and the advertising. The first concert was in 2006. There was no entrance fee, but people made donations and bought charity bracelets. He raised more than two hundred fifty pounds ($360). Then Ben sold tickets for the second concert and he made more than six hundred pounds ($865). The third charity event was more successful than the others. It raised over eight hundred pounds ($1150).

Now Ben's charity concerts are getting bigger and raising more money. Famous bands like the Kaiser Chiefs donate prizes for competitions. In 2006, Ben helped to organize a big concert at the Albert Hall in London. The Albert Hall is an enormous venue that seats five thousand people.

Ben started a company called Northern Music Events a few years ago. He says he is learning a lot about organizing concerts and he hopes the business will grow bigger. He says, "In the future, I'd like Northern Music Events to become an official charity."

Ben's successful business and fund raising show that everyone can do something for charity, not just celebrities like Bob Geldof and Bono.

New words

3 ★★ Match the new words (1–7) with the definitions (a–g).

1 venue
2 entrance fee
3 donation
4 charity bracelet
5 enormous
6 official
7 fund raising

a) (adjective) very big
b) (noun) something, often money, you give to a charity
c) (noun) the place where a concert or other event takes place
d) (adjective) approved by the government, not informal
e) (noun) a piece of plastic jewelry sold to raise money for charity
f) (noun) the act of getting money for a charity
g) (noun) money paid for a ticket

Comprehension

4 ★★ Answer *true* (T) or *false* (F).

1 Ben was sick when he was younger. ☐

2 He organized his first charity concert to pay for school. ☐

3 People didn't buy tickets for the first concert. ☐

4 The second concert was less successful than the first one. ☐

5 Lots of people can sit in the Albert Hall. ☐

6 Ben won't organize concerts in the future. ☐

Large numbers

5 ★ Write the numbers.

1 two hundred fifty   <u>250</u>

2 six hundred   _____

3 eight hundred   _____

4 five thousand   _____

Listen

6 ★★ 🎧 3 Listen to Sal and Joe talking about charity events. Check (✓) the things they decide to do.

Concert for Famine Relief

Five hours of rock, pop, and hip-hop music!

Drake Street High School Hall

Saturday, October 6, 4 P.M.

$5.00

School Book Sale

Come along and buy your books for next year.

90% goes to the student selling the book, 10% of all money raised goes to Book Aid.

Friday, October 5, 4:30–5:30

Fun Run

for The Garratt Children's Hospital

Get support for each half-mile you run and give the money to our good cause.

Sunday, October 7 at 10:00 A.M.

Pajama Friday, October 5

For one day only!

Give $1 to WaterAid, the school's charity for this year, and wear your pajamas to school for a day.

	Concert	Book sale	Fun run	Pajama Friday
Sal				
Joe			✓	

Write

7a ★ You are going to a charity event. Make notes in your notebook about it.

What is the event? When? Which charity is it raising money for? What's going to happen? Where? How much are the tickets?

b ★★ On a piece of paper, write a Twitter message to your friends inviting them to your charity event. (Twitter is a social networking service that lets people send messages to friends through their phones. Each message can be only 140 characters, including letters, numbers, spaces, and punctuation.) Use your notes to help you.

Have you ever made dinner?

Vocabulary: Household jobs

1 ★★ Look at the picture and complete the conversation.

Mom: This is terrible! You haven't **1** _done your chores_ !

Sam: Sorry, Mom!

Dad: First, take the dirty plates to the kitchen and

2 _____ .

Greg: OK, I'll do that.

Mom: Greg, while you are in the kitchen, please **3** _____ .  All those dirty

T-shirts are yours!

Dad: Sam, **4** _____  The carpet is a mess.

Sam: OK, Dad.

Mom: Have you **5** _____ yet?

Greg: No, we haven't. Sorry, Mom.

Mom: Well hurry up! After you finish, you can **6** _____ .

Grammar: Present perfect with adverbs of time: _ever, never, already, yet_

2 ★ Choose an adverb and put it in the correct place in each sentence.

     ever
1 Have you won any money? (never / ⓔⓥⓔⓡ)
      ʌ

2 I want to go to the top of the Space Needle.
  We've been there. (never / yet)

3 Have you done your homework? (never / yet)

4 I'm not hungry. I've eaten five sandwiches.
  (yet / already)

5 I've heard my dad sing. (never / ever)

6 Have you listened to music while you do the
  dishes? It makes it more fun! (already / ever)

7 We haven't bought our concert tickets.
  (never / yet)

3 ★★ Look at the pictures. Write present perfect questions and answers.

1 ever / go / London?

no.

Have you ever been to London?

No, I haven't.

2 ever / see / a celebrity in the street?

no / never / see / a celebrity.

_____

_____

3 do / homework / yet?

yes / do / it / already.

_____

_____

4 ever / spend / $500 on a T-shirt?

no / never / have / $500!

_____

_____

5 ever / read / a play by Shakespeare?

yes / read / *Hamlet*.

_____

_____

6 ever / have / a summer job?

yes / have.

_____

_____

Consolidation

4 Jason's friend Claire is coming for lunch. Read the list and write the sentences.
Use the present perfect with *yet* or *already*.

Things to do today!
1 clean the dining room ✓
2 put flowers on the table ✗
3 choose some music ✓
4 make lunch ✓
5 eat lunch ✗
6 go to the movies ✗
7 do the dishes ✗

1 *Jason has already cleaned the dining room.*

2 He _____

3 He _____

4 He _____

5 Claire and Jason _____

_____

6 They _____

7 He _____

I've seen her here before.

Phrases

1a ★ Complete the phrases.

1 t*ake* c*are* o f

2 to h _ _ _ a f _ _ _ _ _

3 to s _ _ _ _ o _ _

4 to be s u _ _ _ _ _ _ d t _

5 T y _ _ _ _ _ !!

b ★★ Now complete the conversations with the correct form of the words and phrases.

Adam: What's wrong? You look upset.

Matt: I just **1** _____ with my brother. He borrowed my jacket and left it at the movie theater.

Adam: Why don't you call and see if it's still there.

Matt: I have a better idea. I'm going to call my brother. He can **2** _____ it.

Rosie: Have you bought the tickets yet?

Jade: No, sorry, I forgot.

Rosie: **3** _____ ! You *always* forget! You were **4** _____ do it this morning. *Please* remember to do it tomorrow.

Jade: I will. I hope they haven't **5** _____ .

Vocabulary: Relationship words and phrases

2 ★ Write the phrases in the chart.

• ~~ask someone~~ • break up • fall in love
• get divorced • get engaged • get married
• get along • go out • make up

with	to	out	from
		ask someone	

3 ★★ Complete the story. Where necessary, use the simple past.

Isaac and Maria had Saturday jobs in the same café. They **1** *got along* so Isaac **2** _____ Maria out. They fell **3** _____ and they were very happy. They argued a lot but they always **4** _____ up. After one very bad fight, they decided to **5** _____ up. This time, they didn't **6** _____ up. They both got **7** _____ to other people. Soon, however, both Isaac and Maria were bored and unhappy so they got **8** _____ from their partners. Ten years later, Isaac and Maria met and **9** _____ again.

Grammar: Present perfect and simple past

4 ★ Write sentences. Use the present perfect or the simple past.

1 they / get married / five years ago.

   They got married five years ago.

2 he / ask / her / out / yet?

   Has he asked her out yet?

3 you / meet / anyone interesting / recently?

   _____

4 they / just / get engaged.

   _____

5 they / get divorced / in 2009?

   _____

6 they / not agree / a date for their wedding / yet.

   _____

5 ★★ Complete the conversations with the present perfect or the simple past form of the verbs.

Conversation 1

A: 1 *Have* you *spoken* (speak) to your boyfriend today?

B: No, but we 2 *spoke* (speak) yesterday.

Conversation 2

C: You look upset. 3 _____ you and Pete _____ (break up)?

D: Yes, we 4 _____ (break up) yesterday.

Conversation 3

E: 5 _____ you ever _____ (fall) in love at first sight?

F: Yes! I 6 _____ (fall) in love with my wife the day we met.

Conversation 4

G: That's a nice ring. 7 _____ you and Pedro _____ (get) engaged?

H: Yes, he 8 _____ (ask) me last month and I said "yes!"

Conversation 5

J: When 9 _____ your parents _____ (get) married?

K: In 1990. They 10 _____ (be) married for a long time.

Conversation 6

L: Mike and Kathy 11 _____ (choose) an engagement ring last Friday.

M: 12 _____ she _____ (wear) it yet?

L: No, she hasn't.

Use your English: Talk about problems

6 ★ Complete the conversations.

Conversation 1

A: 1 Y*ou* l*ook* w*orried* . What's the matter?

B: I lost my sister's MP3 player. I 2 d_____ k_____ w_____ to do.

A: 3 W_____ d_____ y_____ tell her? It's best to be honest.

B: Yes, you're right.

Conversation 2

C: You look 4 u_____ . 5 W_____ t_____ m_____?

D: I'm 6 w_____ about my homework.

C: 7 M_____ you s_____ talk to your teacher.

D: Yes, good idea. I'll do that.

Consolidation

7 Complete the e-mails with the correct form of the verbs in parentheses.

From: Simon   **Sent:** April 3
To: Ed

Hi Ed,
I 1*have been* (be) very busy! I have a new girlfriend. I 2_____ (ask) her out two weeks ago and, so far, we 3_____ (spend) a lot of time together. I 4_____ (already be) to her house. I 5_____ (have) lunch there last Saturday. Life's great!
Simon

From: Ed   **Sent:** April 20
To: Simon

Hi Simon!
How are you? I 6_____ (not hear) from you recently. How's your girlfriend?
Ed

From: Simon   **Sent:** April 21
To: Ed

Ed,
We 7_____ (have) a big fight on April 7 and we 8_____ (not speak) for TWO WEEKS. I 9_____ (not know) what to do.
Simon

From: Ed   **Sent:** April 22
To: Simon

Hi Simon,
Why don't you 10_____ (e-mail) her?
Ed

From: Simon   **Sent:** April 22
To: Belle

Hi Belle.
I miss you. I'm sorry. :(Can I call you tomorrow?
xoxo

Tips that can help

Vocabulary: Family

1 ★ Complete the words.

1 b r o t h e r -in-law

2 d _ _ _ _ _ _ _ _ -in-law

3 f _ _ _ cé

4 _ _ _ _ _ cée

5 sister- _ _ -law

6 s _ _ -in-l _ _

7 stepb _ _ _ _ _ _

8 stepf _ _ _ _ _ _

9 _ _ _ _ psister

2 ★★ Look at the family tree and complete the sentences with family words.

1 Susan was Sylvia's *daughter-in-law* .

2 Peter was Elaine and Andy's

_____ .

3 Andy was Peter's

_____ .

4 Tim is one of Faith's

_____ .

5 Nina is the boys' _____ .

6 Steve is the boys' _____ .

7 Nina's _____ is Sylvia.

8 Faith is Kate's _____ .

9 Faith and Kate are Susan's

_____ .

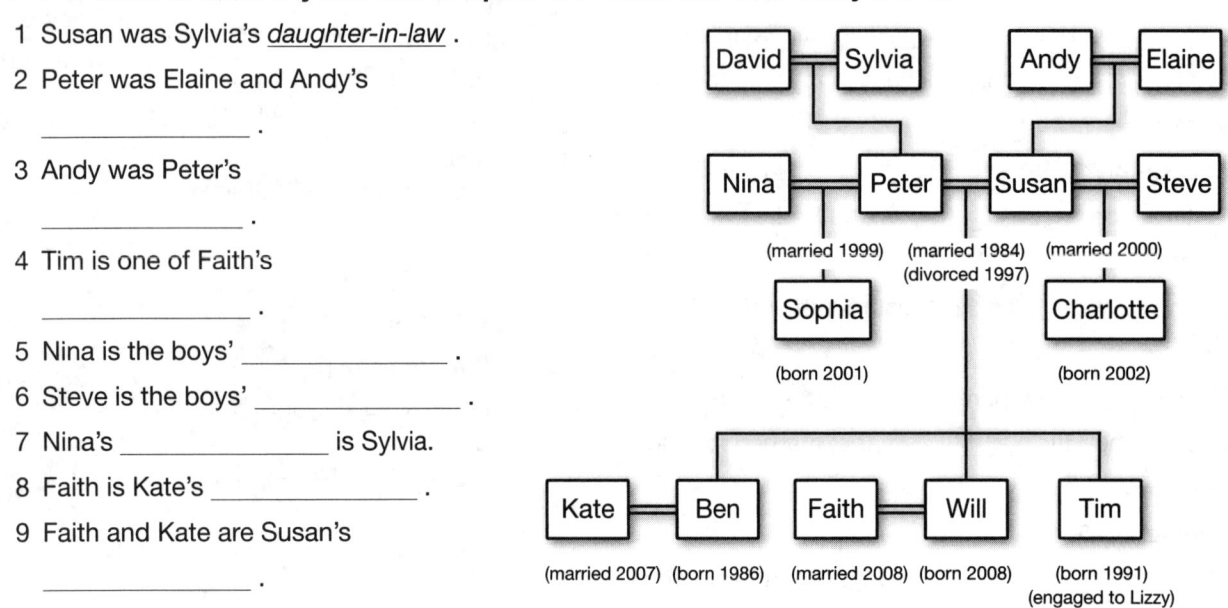

Grammar: Restrictive adjective clauses with *who, that, whose, where*

3 ★ Circle the correct answers.

This is a photo of my brother Gordon's wedding. We're all outside the hotel [1]who/where/that they got married. Gordon is standing next to Claire [2]that/who/whose is now my sister-in-law. His new sister-in-law is the person [3]where/that/whose hat is flying away! Behind everyone you can see the restaurant [4]that/where/whose we had lunch. The meal [5]who/where/that we had was fantastic! After the meal, Gordon and Claire drove to Marina [6]that/where/whose they stayed for their honeymoon.

4 ★★ **Combine the sentences. Make necessary changes.**

1 This is my brother-in-law. He works in a bank. (who)

This is my brother-in-law who works in a bank.

2 This is the dress. My step-sister wore it at my party. (that)

_____

3 They are Mr. and Mrs. Drake. Their daughter married my brother. (whose)

_____

4 Here's your phone. You left it at my house. (that)

_____

5 This is my best friend. She introduced me to my fiancé. (who)

_____

5 ★★ **Check (✓) the correct sentences. Put a relative pronoun in the sentences that need them.**

1 Did you like the girl I introduced you to? ✓

　　　　　where

2 That's the room ⋀ we had the school dance.

3 There's a café near my school sells great smoothies.

4 The boy I met on vacation sent me a text message.

5 Has she told you is the best singer?

6 I got a text message from my cousin lives in Australia.

7 The boy asked her out is named Pete.

Consolidation

6a **Rearrange the words to make sentences.**

1 the where house my grandparents that is live .

That is the house where my grandparents live.

2 is my who lives sister with that the boy next door .

_____

3 married is my mom that to John my who stepfather .

_____

4 sometimes is whose my stepsister that baby I look after .

_____

5 year that last is cat that had the kittens .

_____

6 that is the car my this bought in 1965 grandparents .

_____

b Then match the sentences (1–6) with the photos (a–f).

Extra challenge!

7 ★★★ **Complete the definitions on a separate piece of paper.**

1 A wedding is an event where *two people get married.*

2 A sister-in-law is someone who . . .

3 A boyfriend or girlfriend is someone that . . .

4 A good friend is a person who . . .

5 An only child is one that . . .

6 An engagement ring is something which . . .

Values for living

Problems

Read

1 ★ Match the letters (1 and 2) with the replies (a and b).

1

Dear Teenhelp,
I'm worried about my sister, who is fourteen years old. She is always looking in the mirror. She spends hours brushing her hair and putting on make-up. She thinks she is ugly and fat but she isn't. She's a normal teenager. I'm sixteen and I remember feeling miserable when I was younger but I didn't worry so much. What can I do?
Beth

2

Dear Teenhelp,
I don't know what to do about our fifteen-year-old son. He won't spend any time with us. When he comes home, he goes to his bedroom where he listens to music and uses his computer. His bedroom is messy. When I ask him to clean his room or do the dishes, he gets angry. I understand he needs his own space but I'm worried. What can we do to get our sweet little boy back?
Mrs. Dawson

a

Your son is normal. He's growing up and he is learning to be independent. Most teenagers aren't interested in doing the dishes—they are thinking about their friends and their social life. I'm sorry but your "little boy" will never come back. Be patient and I'm sure your son will become a wonderful young man.

b

This is a common problem. Lots of teenagers worry about how they look and what other people think. Why don't you explain that a lot of people worry about their appearance but it doesn't spoil their lives? Say kind things about your sister's appearance and clothes so she can build some confidence.

New words

2 ★★ Match the new words (1–9) with the definitions (a–i).

1 mirror	a) to fix your hair with a brush
2 brush	b) the way a person looks to other people
3 ugly	c) the things you do outside work or school
4 independent	d) the feeling that you can do something
5 social life	e) not nice to look at
6 common	f) happening often or found everywhere
7 appearance	g) able to do things by yourself
8 confidence	h) a piece of glass where you can see yourself

Comprehension

3 ★★ **Circle the correct answers.**

1 Beth's sister is worried about her ____ .
   a) appearance   b) parents   c) school work

2 Beth's sister's problem is ____ .
   a) imaginary   b) normal   c) unusual

3 Teenhelp suggests that Beth ____ .
   a) tell her sister some jokes
   b) explain that other people worry, too
   c) buy her sister some new clothes

4 Teenhelp thinks Beth can help her sister ____ .
   a) choose nice clothes
   b) find a boyfriend
   c) to be happier

5 Mrs. Dawson has written because ____ .
   a) her son is sweet
   b) her son spends too much time at home
   c) she is worried

6 Mrs. Dawson's son ____ .
   a) never comes home after school
   b) won't spend time with his parents
   c) wants to leave home

7 Teenhelp thinks most teenagers don't want to do
   the dishes because they ____ .
   a) have a lot of homework
   b) listen to too much music
   c) are thinking about other things

Listen

Learning Strategy: Listening for the main idea
Remember! Listen to the whole recording first,
to get a general idea of the meaning. Then listen
again for details.

4 ★ (4) **Listen and circle the correct answers.**

1 Who's talking?
   a) father and daughter   b) two friends

2 What are they talking about?
   a) Mimi had an argument at home.
   b) Fred had an argument at home.

5 ★★ **Listen again and circle the correct
answers.**

1 Mimi ____ with her dad.
   a) breaks up   b) gets along   c) has arguments

2 Last week Mimi's dad was angry about ____ .
   a) her bedroom   b) her homework
   c) the dishes

3 Mimi ____ having a messy bedroom.
   a) doesn't enjoy   b) hates   c) likes

4 Fred thinks Mimi's father is ____ .
   a) bossy   b) right   c) wrong

5 Mimi's dad is also angry because she ____ .
   a) cooked a meal   b) didn't cook dinner
   c) didn't do the dishes

6 Fred's advice is to ____ with her father.
   a) have a fight   b) get along   c) make up

Write

6a ★ **Your friend is worried about some tests
next month. Your friend has asked for your help.
Read the suggestions and add two more ideas.**

1 write a study schedule

2 do some reviewing every day

3 _____

4 _____

b ★★ **Now, on a piece of paper, write an e-mail
to your friend. Use your ideas and the phrases
in the box.**

- I think you should . . . • I usually . . .
- Maybe you should . . . • Why don't you . . .

From: ____
To: ____

Hi!
I know you are worried about your exams.

Turn right.

Vocabulary: Places in town

1 ★ Match the pictures (1–9) with the places in town (a–k). There are two extra places.

 1 | *k*

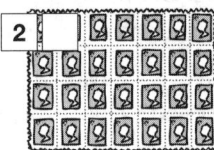 2

 3

 4

 5

 6

7

8

9

a) bookstore

b) computer store

c) factory

d) gas station

e) police station

f) post office

g) shopping center

h) sports complex

i) square

j) tourist information center

k) zoo

2 ★★ Write words to complete the sentences.

1 I'm going to the b o o k s t o r e. I want to buy a magazine.

2 Let's go to the _ u _ _ _ _. There's a dinosaur exhibit that looks cool.

3 Leave the car in the _ a _ _ _ _ _ l _ _ while we go shopping.

4 I've never seen a Shakespeare play in a _ _ e _ _ _ _.

5 There's a Picasso exhibit at the art _ _ _ l _ _ _.

6 She's going to the p _ _ _ _ _ _ _ to buy some medicine.

7 What time does your train leave the _ _ _ _ i _ _?

8 I want to borrow a book from the _ _ b _ _ _ _.

9 My grandmother buys all her clothes at the _ _ _ l.

10 Let's stop at the _ _ n _ to get some money.

Vocabulary: Directions

3 ★ Match the places on the map (1–7) with the phrases (a–g).

a) at the end of the street

b) cross the street | *1*

c) turn left

d) go past the station

e) go straight at the traffic light

f) across from the bank

g) turn right

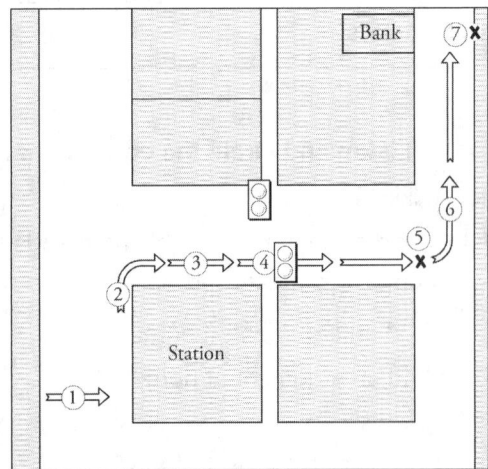

4 ★★ Complete the instructions.

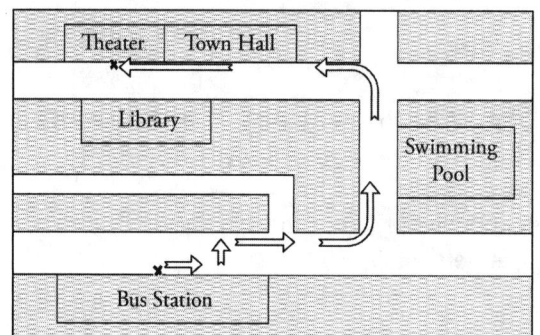

Go 1 _right_ out of the bus station and 2 c_____ the
street. Take the second 3 _____ . Go 4 _____
the swimming pool and turn 5 _____ .
Go 6 _____ the town hall. The theater is
7 _____ the library, 8 _____ to the town hall.

Use your English: Ask for and give directions

5 ★ Complete the conversations with the phrases in the box.

> • Can you tell me how to get • You're welcome
> • How do I get there, please
> • Sorry to bother you but • Thanks very much
> • ~~Where's the swimming pool~~ • You can't miss it

Conversation 1

A: Excuse me. 1 _Where's the swimming pool_ ?

B: It's next to the sports complex.

A: 2 _____ to the sports
   complex, please?

B: Yes, go down Mill Road and it's on the left.

   3 _____ .

A: 4 _____ .

Conversation 2

C: 5 _____ where's the
   nearest bank, please?

D: It's on 12ᵗʰ Street.

C: 6 _____ ?

D: Go down Broadway and turn left. It's across from
   the library.

C: Thank you.

D: 7 _____ .

6 ★★ Complete the conversations.

Conversation 1

A: How do I 1 _get_ to the station, please?

B: 2 _____ left at the first traffic light, go 3 _____
   to the end of the road and 4 _____ right.

A: Thank you.

B: No 5 _____ .

Conversation 2

C: 6 _____ me. 7 _____ the nearest café, please?

D: It's on Fulton Street.

C: Can you tell me 8 _____ there, please?

D: Cross the street at the traffic light and turn right.
   You can't 9 _____ it.

Consolidation

7 Look at the map and complete the directions.

A Come out of the station and cross Station Road.
   Turn right and walk to the traffic light. Turn left
   and the 1 _____ is on your right.

B Leave the station and turn left. Go down Station
   Road and turn right at the parking lot. Continue
   on Green Road—the 2 _____ is at the end
   of the road on the right.

C Go down the road across from the bank. After the
   second traffic light, take the second left.
   The 3 _____ is on the left.

D When you leave the post office, go left and left
   again. The 4 _____ is at the end of the street.

E Go left out of the hospital and take the first right.
   Go straight and the 5 _____ is the first
   place on the left.

It's too difficult to park.

Vocabulary: Transportation

1 ★ Find six more transportation words.

p	a	b	c	w	m	i	n
l	a	i	c	t	o	b	e
t	m	k	a	r	n	s	v
r	d	e	r	a	o	k	f
a	h	c	f	q	r	b	e
i	v	a	n	u	a	p	r
n	o	e	s	h	i	p	r
y	b	u	s	z	l	c	y

2 ★★ Label the pictures.

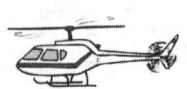  

1 _helicopter_   2 _____   3 _____

4 _____   5 _____   6 _____

Grammar: *too* + adjective / adverb + *to*, (*not*) + adjective / adverb + *enough to*

3 ★ Choose the correct answers.

1 Jake is six feet tall. He's _a_ be a basketball star.
  (a) tall enough to   b) not short enough to
  c) too tall to

2 Nell and Meg are good swimmers but they are
  ___ win in the Olympics.
  a) too fast to   b) old enough to
  c) not good enough to

3 You're thirteen years old! You're ___ ride a
  motorcycle!
  a) young enough to   b) not young enough to
  c) too young to

4 I read the book ___ remember it.
  a) too quickly to   b) quickly enough to
  c) not quickly enough to

4 ★★ Write the sentences. Use the words in the box with *too* + *to* or (*not*) + *enough to*.

> • expensive • late • not old
> • ~~not rich~~ • tall

1 they / pay for a cab
  They aren't rich enough
  to pay for a cab.

2 they / go in
  _____
  _____

3 they / get on the boat
  _____
  _____

4 he / see
  _____
  _____

5 the tickets / buy
  _____
  _____

Vocabulary: Adjectives and nouns of measurement

5 ★ Write the words in the chart.

> • age • deep • distance • expensive • high
> • length • size • ~~speed~~ • width

	Adjective	Noun
1	fast	*speed*
2		cost
3		depth
4	long	
5	wide	
6		height
7	big	
8	old	
9	far	

6 ★★ Complete the text with some of the words from Exercise 5.

Ladies and gentlemen, look to your right and you can see the Clock Tower. Big Ben is the bell at the top. The tower is more than a hundred years **1** _old_ . It is 315 feet **2** _____ . The bell in the clock is very **3** _____ and heavy: its **4** _____ is 7.2 feet and its width is 9.5 feet. The **5** _____ of the clock is impressive: each face is 23 feet **6** _____ . On the right is the River Thames. The boats can't travel very fast—the top **7** _____ is about 15 miles per hour. The Thames is about 656 feet wide here and the **8** _____ changes at different times of the day. On your left is the famous Savoy Hotel. I don't know how much a room costs, but I know it's very **9** _____ !

Consolidation

7 Some tourists are talking about New York's Metropolitan Museum of Art.
Match the beginnings (1–7) with the endings (a–g).

1 It's great but
2 It's boring;
3 The things in the store were
4 Our guide
5 The restaurant
6 It was
7 Tomorrow we're coming

a) cheap enough to buy presents for all my friends.
b) early enough to be in first.
c) it's too big to see in a day.
d) spoke too quickly for me to understand everything.
e) there isn't enough for children to do.
f) too crowded to see everything.
g) was too expensive to take four kids for lunch.

Extra challenge!

8a ★★★ Make notes about your capital city.

• Transportation: *buses very slow but very cheap, cabs cheap and fast*

• Museums: _____

• Art galleries: _____

• Famous buildings: _____

b ★★★ Now, on a piece of paper, write a paragraph describing your capital city for a tourist.

4c There's too much pollution.

Vocabulary: Count and non-count nouns

1 ★ **Choose the correct answers.**

1 There __a__ in our local rivers.
   (a) is pollution   b) are pollutions

2 ___ moving into town in the winter.
   a) Bears are   b) Bear is

3 The people in the town asked vets
   for ___ .
   a) advices   b) advice

4 The city collects our ___ every week.
   a) garbages   b) garbage

5 Recycle ___ and save ___ .
   a) paper / trees   b) papers / tree

2 ★★ **There is a mistake in each sentence. Find it and correct it.**

1 There are thousands of ~~building~~ in Seattle.

   There are thousands of buildings in
   Seattle.

2 Be careful, there are ice on the roads.

   _____

   _____

3 Are the food good in Spain?

   _____

4 Can we have two glasses of waters, please?

   _____

   _____

5 There are lots of interesting information about bears.

   _____

   _____

6 How often do you listen to musics?

   _____

Grammar: *too many, too much, not enough*

3 ★ **Complete the sentences with *too many, too much,* or *not enough.***

1 Tokyo is very crowded because *too many* people live and work in the city.

2 I have _____ homework this evening: math, French, geography, history, and science.

3 We're late! There's _____ time to walk to the movie.

4 The streets are always very busy because there are _____ cars in the city.

5 There are so many things to see in Seattle. There's _____ time to see everything.

4 ★★ **Complete the conversation.**

Mrs. Richards: I'm not sure I want to live here. There
   1 *are too many* cars and there **2** _____
   noise from that busy street.

Mr. Richards: Do you like the apartment buildings?

Mrs. Richards: No, I don't. Look at the bags of garbage! There
   3 _____ garbage cans.

Mr. Richards: I agree but I like the dogs.

Mrs. Richards: I hate dogs! There **4** _____ dogs.

Mr. Richards: Well, there's a tree. You like trees.

Mrs. Richards: OK, there's one tree. There **5** _____ trees
   and there **6** _____ grass.

Mr. Richards: It's near my job in the factory.

Mrs. Richards: I know, there **7** _____ pollution.

Mr. Richards: Do you like anything?

Mrs. Richards: No, I don't!

Grammar: Indefinite pronouns *some-, any-, no-, every-* + *thing, where, one, body*

5 ★ Circle the correct choices.

1 *Everyone / Anyone* wanted to see the polar bears.

2 *Anybody / Nobody* wants to live in a polluted city.

3 Does *someone / anyone* know how much pollution there is from cars?

4 You see old plastic bags *anywhere / everywhere*.

5 Do you know *anything / anywhere* about global warming?

6 I want to live *nowhere / somewhere* near a movie theater and lots of restaurants.

7 There's *nowhere / nothing* to go on the weekends.

8 Do you ever walk *anywhere / everywhere*?

9 *Everything / Anything* I buy is environmentally friendly.

6 ★★ Complete the article with the correct pronouns.

Every time you turn on the radio or TV, you hear ¹*something* about pollution or global warming. It's very depressing, but is there ² _____ we can do about it?

Yes! There are lots of things we can do. ³ _____ should recycle things. In most towns there is ⁴ _____ you can take glass bottles, cans, and old newspapers. You can start a recycling project at your school. I'm sure ⁵ _____ will want to help. Start by asking your teachers for ⁶ _____ to put the paper and cans in.

Remember, ⁷ _____ we do adds to our carbon footprint, so try to make sensible choices. Even the smallest change is better than doing ⁸ _____ . For example, before you drive ⁹ _____ , think about walking instead!

Consolidation

7 Complete the article. Use words from the boxes. There is an extra word in each box.

Paragraph 1
• anybody • anywhere • everywhere • nobody
• not enough • ~~too many~~ • too much

Animals in England

In the past, there were about 4,000 birds in London's Trafalgar Square. The government said that there were ¹*too many* birds. ² _____ you looked, you saw one! The birds damaged buildings and the City of London spent ³ _____ money cleaning them. The government made it illegal for ⁴ _____ to feed the birds ⁵ _____ in the square. Now there are about 200 birds in the square; enough for the photographers, but ⁶ _____ to cause problems.

Paragraph 2
• no one • somebody • something • sometimes
• somewhere • too much

⁷ _____ people driving in the north of England see ⁸ _____ that surprises them: wallabies! ⁹ _____ brought the animals from Australia many years ago but they escaped in the 1930s. They didn't leave to find ¹⁰ _____ warmer, they stayed in the area. They nearly all died in a very cold winter forty years ago. Luckily, there are still some there, but ¹¹ _____ knows exactly how many.

Focus on Hong Kong

Read

1 ★ Read and complete the article about Hong Kong with the topic sentences (a–e).

a) A lot of movies are made in Hong Kong.

b) Hong Kong is in a subtropical location

c) Hong Kong is in southeastern China.

d) ~~Hong Kong is opposite Los Angeles~~

e) The tourist industry is important in Hong Kong.

¹*Hong Kong is opposite Los Angeles*—but there is more than 6,831 miles of ocean between them! The two cities share lots of things: both have a movie industry, tourism, lots of manufacturing, too much pollution, and hill fires in the fall.

² _____ It's a small area with more than two hundred islands. Some islands don't have anyone living on them, but the city is very crowded. There isn't enough space to build houses so there are lots of skyscrapers.

³ _____ There is something for everyone to enjoy: a boat ride in the harbor, a trip to the highest mountain in the city, shopping, eating in the fantastic restaurants, and going to Hong Kong Disneyland.

⁴ _____ It is famous for its pop and action movies. Bruce Lee and Jackie Chan are well known all over the world for their exciting kung fu movies. There is an important and popular film festival every year.

⁵ _____ so there is a problem with typhoons in the summer months. The wind speed in a typhoon can be as much as 100 miles per hour. These terrible storms can damage buildings, cause landslides and floods, sink ships, and pull trees out of the ground. During a typhoon, everything closes and everybody goes home because it's too dangerous to be outside.

New words

2 ★ **Match the new words (1–5) with the definitions (a–e).**

1 hill fire
2 skyscraper
3 kung fu
4 typhoon
5 landslide

a) a very tall building
b) old Chinese fighting using hands and feet
c) a fire in the countryside
d) when a lot of earth and rocks suddenly fall down a hill
e) very bad weather with strong wind and heavy rain

Comprehension

3 ★★ **Answer** *true* **(T) or** *false* **(F).**

1 Los Angeles is near Hong Kong. ☐
2 There is nothing the same in the two cities. ☐
3 Hong Kong is near the sea. ☐
4 You can get good food in Hong Kong restaurants. ☐
5 There isn't a theme park in Hong Kong. ☐
6 Typhoons cause serious problems. ☐

Listen

4 ★ 🎧 5 **Listen and circle the correct answers.**

1 The speaker is talking to *tourists* / *local people*.

2 The speaker tells them about *a famous site* / *things they can do*.

3 The speaker *will* / *won't* go with the people.

5 ★★ **Listen again and circle the correct answers.**

1 The speaker says Central and Nathan Roads have the best ____ .
a) restaurants   b) shops   c) markets

2 The things in the markets are ____ .
a) cheap   b) boring   c) all the same

3 At first, the market sellers ask for ____ .
a) too much money   b) not enough money
c) the right price

4 There are ____ places to eat in Hong Kong.
a) a few   b) not enough   c) lots of

5 There is a ____ to the top of the mountain.
a) tram   b) train   c) tube

6 The mountain is about ____ high.
a) 1,312 feet   b) 312 feet
c) 1 mile

Write

> **Learning Strategy: Organize paragraphs by topic**
>
> **Remember!** Organize your writing in paragraphs with different topics. You can start each new paragraph with a "topic sentence." This tells the reader the main topic of the paragraph.

6a ★ **Complete these topic sentences so they are true for where you live.**

• I live in a town/city called _____ .

• The best things about my town/city are:

_____

_____

• The worst things about my town/city are:

_____

_____

b ★★ **Now write two pieces of information to go with each topic sentence.**

For example,

I live in a town called _____

- *small town*

- *near the ocean*

7 ★★ **On a piece of paper, write three paragraphs about where you live.**

We've gotten along well since we met.

Vocabulary: Collocations with *make* and *do*

1 ★ Complete the sentences with *make* or *do*.

1 Can you *make* some breakfast, please?

2 I always try to _____ my best.

3 Please _____ a decision! Do you want tea or coffee?

4 I help my parents _____ the laundry on Saturdays.

5 Let's stay home this evening and _____ nothing.

6 Your hair is too long! _____ an appointment for a haircut.

7 Please don't _____ a mess. I just cleaned the house.

8 Sally is very social. She _____ friends easily.

2 ★★ Complete the sentences with the correct form of *make* or *do*.

I don't like **1** *doing* homework and, until this year, I always **2** *did* it at the last minute.

No, you can't **3** _____ lunch tomorrow. Last time, you **4** _____ a big mess in the kitchen.

What are the children doing? They **5** _____ a lot of noise.

6 _____ you _____ any homework before you went to bed?

Since September, I **7** _____ some exercise every day and it **8** _____ a difference in my health.

Next month I **9** _____ money working in a café.

My grandmother **10** _____ ten cups of tea a day!

I failed my music test because I **11** _____ too many mistakes.

Grammar: Present perfect with *for* and *since*

3 ★ Put *for* or *since* in the correct place in each sentence.

1 Jenna and Polly have been friends ʌ they met.
   since

2 Her family has lived in Seattle three months.

3 My cousins have been here a week.

4 Have you spoken to Jenna last week?

5 They have been on the bus two o'clock.

6 Jenna hasn't looked at her science book two days.

7 Polly has lived in Seattle she was a baby.

8 Jenna hasn't watched soccer she came to the U.S.

4 ★★ **Write two sentences for each picture. Use the present perfect with *for* and *since*.**

1 Great Blue Heron / be / the official city bird

+ 2003
+ many years

_____

_____

_____

2 Dahlia / be / the official city flower

+ 1913
+ a century

_____

_____

_____

3 The Seattle Space Needle / welcome / visitors

+ it was built in 1962
+ decades

_____

_____

_____

_____

4 Jenna / take / the monorail / every day

+ she moved here
+ eight months

_____

_____

_____

5 People who live in Seattle / recycle / newspapers

+ 1988
+ more than 20 years

_____

_____

_____

_____

Consolidation

5 Complete the conversation with the correct form of the verbs in the box.

• do • have • make (×2) • not do • ~~not know~~
• work

Customer: Hi, Calvin. I **1** *didn't know* you had a job. How long have you worked here?

Calvin: I **2** _____ this job since I was fifteen. So, I **3** _____ here for a year.

Customer: What's it like?

Calvin: At lunchtime, I **4** _____ lots of sandwiches and cups of coffee. After lunchtime, I **5** _____ the dishes. Luckily, I **6** _____ the dishes at home since I got the job!

Customer: Do you enjoy it?

Calvin: Yes, I do. Although, it feels like I **7** _____ a thousand cups of coffee since this morning.

How long have you been waiting?

Phrases

1 ★ Complete the conversation with the phrases in the box.

> • for ages • taking turns
> • ~~What on earth~~ • worth all this trouble

Jo: Hi! **1** *What on earth* have you been doing?
I've been calling you **2** _____ but you
haven't answered.

Mark: Hi, I've been trying to speak to someone
at the ticket office.

Jo: For five hours?

Mark: Yes, Karl and I have been **3** _____ on
the telephone since nine o'clock this morning!

Jo: What do you want tickets for?

Mark: The jazz and blues festival.

Jo: I hope it's **4** _____ .

Mark: Yes, it will be.

Vocabulary: Phrasal verbs with *look*

**2a ★★ Match the phrasal verbs (1–4) with the
definitions (a–d).**

1 look at

2 look for

3 look forward to

4 look up

a) to try to find information in
a book or on the Internet

b) to be excited or happy
about something that is
going to happen

c) to turn your eyes to
something so you can see it

d) to try to find something

**b ★★ Now complete the sentences with the
correct form of the phrasal verbs.**

1 You can _____ the date of the next concert
on the band's website.

2 I always _____ doing nothing on Sundays.

3 He _____ his friends in the line but he
couldn't find them.

4 Can you _____ the tickets and tell me what
time the concert starts, please?

Grammar: Present perfect continuous with *for* and *since*

3 ★★ Write two sentences for each picture. Use the present perfect continuous with *for* and *since*.

1 How long has she been reading?

She's been reading for thirty-five minutes.

She's been reading since ten-thirty.

2 How long haven't they been speaking?

They _____

_____

01:15

3 How long have they been watching TV?

They _____

_____

4 How long has the baby been crying?

He _____ ages.

JUNE
M Tu W Th F Sa Su

JULY
M Tu W Th F Sa Su

5 How long has he been swimming?

He _____

_____

6 How long hasn't she been running?

She _____

4 ★★ **Complete the interview with the present perfect continuous form of the verbs in the box.**

> • eat • listen • make • talk • try • use • wait (x2)

TV reporter: Good evening everyone. I'm here outside the Seattle Memorial Stadium. Fans **1** *have been waiting* on line since Monday night for tickets to see Lady Gaga. Let's talk to Erin and her boyfriend Gil. Hi. How long have you been waiting?

Gil: We arrived on Monday morning. We **2** _____ _____ for three days.

TV reporter: What have you been doing to pass the time?

Gil: We **3** _____ to music.

Erin: I **4** _____ to other people in the line.

TV reporter: What about food? What **5** _____ you _____ ?

Erin: Our moms **6** _____ pizza and bringing it here every day.

TV reporter: And what about going to the bathroom?

Gil: We **7** _____ the bathrooms in the park.

TV reporter: You must be big Lady Gaga fans.

Erin: Yes, I **8** _____ to get tickets for a concert for a long time. It's been impossible. I decided that this is the only way.

Consolidation

5 **Complete the blog with the present perfect continuous form of the verbs in the box.**

> • call • listen • look for • not eat
> • sleep • ~~travel~~ • write

Guitar Man's blog

I'm really tired tonight. The band is working very hard. We **1***have been traveling* for seven weeks and we **2** _____ on the bus between concerts. We're all feeling lousy because we **3** _____ good food.

The band **4** _____ a new keyboard player since last December. We put an ad in *Rock* newspaper and a bunch of people sent in audition songs. I **5** _____ to the songs but we haven't found anyone yet. I **6** _____ friends for ideas since last weekend.

I **7** _____ lots of new songs since I broke up with my girlfriend. They will be for sale on our website next year.

Goodnight!

Grammar: Present perfect and continuous with *for* and *since*

1 ★ Choose the correct answers.

1 The chicken must be ready. It __b__ for two hours.
   a) has roasted (b) has been roasting)

2 How long ___ her own bread?
   a) has Nell been making   b) has Nell made

3 ___ the dishes yet?
   a) Have you been doing   b) Have you done

4 Greg ___ much recently because he's trying to lose weight.
   a) hasn't eaten   b) hasn't been eating

5 I'm tired. ___ for three hours.
   a) I've been cooking   b) I've cooked

2 ★★ Make sentences. Use the present perfect or continuous.

1 the burger shack / sell / burgers since 2001
   The burger shack has been selling burgers since 2001.

2 the burger shack / sell / three million burgers
   The burger shack has sold three million burgers.

3 I / invent / lots of different sandwiches
   _____

4 I / invent / sandwiches / for a long time
   _____

5 my grandmother / collect / five hundred recipes
   _____

6 my brother / cook / since he was five years old
   _____

7 my sister / not cook / anything / since January
   _____

8 I / never like / vegetables
   _____

9 my sister / like / prawns / since she tried them in Portugal
   _____

10 you / ever make / meal for ten people?
   _____

Vocabulary: Food and drink; cooking verbs

3 ★ Circle the words that don't belong.

1 sugar   honey   (onion)   chocolate
2 banana   cheese   peach   grape
3 chicken   lamb   beef   meat
4 pasta   potato   apple   rice
5 pea   cream   yogurt   butter
6 cheesecake   salt   dessert   ice cream
7 tomato   cucumber   vinegar   lettuce

4 ★ Write the instructions. Use a verb (1–9) and a food (a–i) with *a*, *an*, or *some*.

1 fry	6 pour	a) apple	f) egg
2 grate	7 roast	b) bread	g) juice
3 grill	8 slice	c) butter	h) lamb
4 ~~heat~~	9 spread	d) cheese	i) ~~milk~~
5 peel		e) chicken	

1 *heat some milk*   2 _____   3 _____

  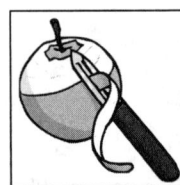

4 _____   5 _____   6 _____

7 _____   8 _____   9 _____

Use your English: Offer, accept or refuse, persuade

5 ★ **Circle the correct answer.**

Conversation 1

A: 1 (Would) / Do you like a cup of coffee?

B: No, 2 please / thanks. I just had a cup of tea.

Conversation 2

C: Would you 3 want / like a cheese sandwich?

D: Yes, 4 please / thanks. 5 I'd love / I'm loving one.

Conversation 3

E: 6 Will / Would you like some cookies?

F: Thanks, 7 that / they would be great.

Conversation 4

G: Would you 8 like / want some ice cream?

H: 9 Yes / No, I'm fine, thanks.

G: Oh, go 10 ahead / up. It's delicious.

Conversation 5

J: 11 Are / Do you want some orange juice?

K: No, thanks.

J: Are you 12 already / sure? It's delicious.

6 ★★ **Write the short conversations. Use different phrases each time.**

Conversation 1

A: offer some fruit _____

B: accept _____

Conversation 2

C: offer a glass of bottled water _____

_____

D: refuse, you just had some juice _____

_____

Conversation 3

E: offer some dessert _____

F: refuse _____

E: persuade, say it's delicious _____

_____

Conversation 4

G: offer a pizza _____

H: accept _____

Consolidation

7 **Complete the conversation with the present perfect or continuous form of the verbs in the box.**

- leave • make • not do • not work
- talk • want

Mom: The kitchen is a terrible mess! There is food everywhere. 1 *Have* you *been making* pizza?

Sam: Yes, I have.

Mom: Why 2 _____ you _____ the dishes yet? You 3 _____ tomato and cheese everywhere!

Sam: Sorry, Mom. Grandma just called. I 4 _____ to her for half an hour.

Mom: Why did she call?

Sam: Her laptop 5 _____ since Wednesday.

Mom: Is it working now?

Sam: No, it isn't. I think she broke it.

Mom: Oh, no.

Sam: It's not a problem. She 6 _____ a new one for a long time.

Extra challenge!

8 ★★★ **Complete the sentences with your own ideas.**

1 I've never done my homework *in the bathroom* .

2 I've been taking tests since _____ .

3 I haven't made mistakes in my _____ classes since elementary school.

4 I've been looking forward to _____ since the beginning of school.

5 I've never taken care of my neighbor's _____ .

6 I've loved _____ since I was little.

7 I've been eating lots of _____ for the last few weeks.

8 I haven't eaten _____ since I was little.

Space travel

Read

1 ★ Read the text and choose the correct answers.

1 The text is about ___ .

  a) a spacecraft b) exploring space c) an astronaut

2 The text tells you ___ information.

  a) scientific b) general c) unusual

3 The best title is ___ .

  a) *Why people go into space* b) *Famous science fiction writers* c) *A short history of space travel*

> **Learning Strategy: Using context clues**
> **Remember!** Use clues to guess the meaning of new words. First, decide what part of speech the word is (e.g. a verb, noun, or adjective). Then guess what it means from the context. You can check the meaning in a dictionary later.

For thousands of years, people have looked at the night sky and dreamed about traveling in space.

A

When space travel was still a dream, scientists studied the constellations and learned about our solar system. In the sixteenth century a Polish astronomer, Copernicus, said the Earth orbited the sun. This was a radical idea at the time. Then, a hundred years later, a British scientist named Newton discovered gravity. The ideas of these two men and other great scientists have helped the work of modern space scientists.

B

In the twentieth century, improvements in technology helped scientists test their theories. Engineers have built powerful engines so spacecraft can accelerate more quickly. Better acceleration means spacecraft can escape from the Earth's gravity.

C

In the 1950s, the Russians and the Americans sent unmanned spacecraft to orbit the Earth. Then, in 1961, Yuri Alexeyevich Gagarin became the first man in space. The Russians won that part of the space race but the Americans won the next part: in 1969 Neil Armstrong stepped onto the moon. Since the 1960s, hundreds of people have flown in space.

D

The International Space Station has been orbiting the Earth since the 1990s. It has a crew of astronauts and scientists from all over the world. On this flying space laboratory scientists have been doing research, like studying the effects of weightlessness on the human body.

New words

2a ★ Write *verb*, *noun*, or *adjective*.

1 solar system   *noun*

2 astronomer   _____

3 orbit(ed)   _____

4 radical   _____

5 gravity   _____

6 theory   _____

7 powerful   _____

8 accelerate   _____

9 unmanned   _____

b ★★ Then match the new words (1–9) with the definitions (a–i).

a) very strong

b) with no people in it

c) the force that makes things fall to the ground

d) to go faster

e) an idea that tries to explain something

f) a scientist who studies stars and planets

g) the sun and the planets that go round it

h) new and very different

i) to travel around something in space

Comprehension

3 ★ Match the pictures (1–6) with the paragraphs (A–D).

A _____

B _____

C _____

D _____

4 ★★ Answer *true* (T) or *false* (F).

1 People weren't interested in space before the twentieth century. ☐

2 Before Newton, people didn't understand gravity. ☐

3 Only Copernicus and Newton helped modern space scientists. ☐

4 In the nineteenth century, engines were powerful enough for space travel. ☐

5 People didn't go into space in the 1950s. ☐

6 In the 1960s, the Americans and the Russians raced to put the first person on the moon. ☐

7 The International Space Station has been orbiting the Earth for about thirty years. ☐

Listen

5 ★ 🎧 Listen and circle the correct answers.

1 This is a telephone *conversation / message*.

2 The information is about *the Space Theme Park / the Education Center*.

6 ★★ Listen again and match the callers with the number they need: 1, 2, 3, 4, or 5.

Caller A is a journalist with some questions about the space race exhibition. ☐

Caller B wants to ask if the park is suitable for disabled visitors. ☐

Caller C is a teacher. She wants to arrange a school visit. ☐

Caller D wants to buy tickets for his family. ☐

7 ★★ Which two numbers can you press to speak to a real person?

_____

Write

8 ★★ You are on a school trip to the Space Theme Park. It's lunchtime and you are in the computer room in the education center. On a piece of paper, write an e-mail to your friend about the visit.

You have
• seen models of the solar system
• traveled in a virtual spacecraft
• watched a movie about Mars

You haven't
• visited The Story of the Space Race exhibition yet

From:	
To:	

Hi!

I'm at the Space Theme Park. This morning . . .

He used to play in a band.

Grammar: *used to*

1 ★ Rearrange the words to make sentences.

1 listen people to to music on cassettes used .

People used to listen to music on cassettes.

2 use personal people have computers did to ?

_____

3 use didn't to go people snowboarding .

_____

4 used phones to very be big cell .

_____

5 to cost did much use how a computer ?

_____

6 used cameras use film to .

_____

2 ★★ Make sentences. Use the correct form of *used to*.

1 he / wear shorts

He used to wear shorts.

2 she / not wear make-up

_____

3 they / play with toys

_____

4 they / not have cell phones

_____

5 their parents / ride bicycles

_____

6 their parents / not have a car

_____

7 they / get along with each other

_____

8 they / not argue with each other

_____

3 ★★ Look at the pictures in Exercise 2. Make questions about the twins using the correct form of *used to* and write short answers.

1 he / have blond hair?

Did he use to have blond hair?

Yes, he did.

2 she / have short hair?

_____

_____

3 be / a tree in the yard?

_____

_____

4 he / have a bicycle?

_____

_____

5 she / wear jeans?

_____

_____

6 their parents / have a car?

_____

_____

Use Your English: Confirm and clarify Information

4 ★ **Complete the conversations. Use *what*, *when*, *where*, or *who*.**

1 My parents used to live on a boat.
   Your parents used to live _where_ ?

2 I wake up at 5 A.M. to milk the cows before school.
   You wake up _____ to do _____?

3 Next year my cousins are taking a vacation to Africa.
   _____ is taking a vacation to Africa?

4 Every Sunday my family has hamburgers and milk shakes for breakfast.
   Your family has _____ for breakfast?

5 Mr. Kim said our history test is tomorrow.
   He said our history test is _____? Oh no!

6 I've been working at the police station since I was twelve.
   You've been working _____ since you were twelve?

5 ★★ **Ask questions to clarify and confirm information. There are at least two questions for each sentence.**

1 Can you believe Principal Rogers used to be a rap star?
   Principal Rogers used to be a what?
   Who used to be a rap star?

2 My parents got married on New Year's Eve at the top of the Eiffel Tower.
   _____
   _____

3 That store has been closed since January.
   _____
   _____

4 Andrew and Millie are starting a new band called The Refrigerators.
   _____
   _____

5 The bus driver got lost going from the hotel to the stadium.
   _____
   _____

6 Can you help me carry this sofa upstairs to my apartment? I live on the fifth floor.
   _____
   _____

Consolidation

6 Complete the phone conversation. Write questions to confirm or clarify information or use the correct form of *used to*.

Bill: Hi, Maria. How's it going?

Maria: Great! I'm at my sister's wedding.

Bill: You're **1** _____ (?) ?

Maria: At my sister's wedding!

Bill: Awesome. Who did she marry?

Maria: His name is Thunder Rock.

Bill: His name is **2** _____ (?)?

Maria: It's a little strange. But she's in a band and . . .

Bill: I thought she **3** _____ (be) a teacher!

Maria: She did. But she hasn't taught since she won National Idol.

Bill: She hasn't taught since **4** _____ (?)?

Maria: She won the competition about two years ago. Then she met her husband, and they started a band.

Bill: How did they meet?

Maria: They met at a concert. She **5** _____ (not/want) to get married. But after she met Thunder, she changed her mind. Actually, I think you **6** _____ (go) to school with him. His name **7** _____ (be) Henry Tomlin.

Bill: Did he **8** _____ (live) on Main Street?

Maria: Yes!

Bill: That's funny. We **9** _____ (take) piano lessons together. He was great!

Maria: Really? **10** _____ he **11** _____ (sing) too?

Bill: No, he was too shy.

Maria: Too **12** _____ (?) I guess he's changed.

Bill: I guess so. Well, have fun. See you soon.

Vocabulary: Action verbs

1 ★ Circle the correct answers.

1 You can't *sink* / (swim) here.

2 Be careful, don't *trip* / *slip*.

3 Don't *dive* / *fall* here. The water isn't deep enough.

4 Don't drive your car into the river and *fall* / *sink*.

5 Don't *fall* / *jump* off your bike.

2 ★★ Complete the instructions with words from the box.

> • climb (×2) • dive • jump • push • run • swim

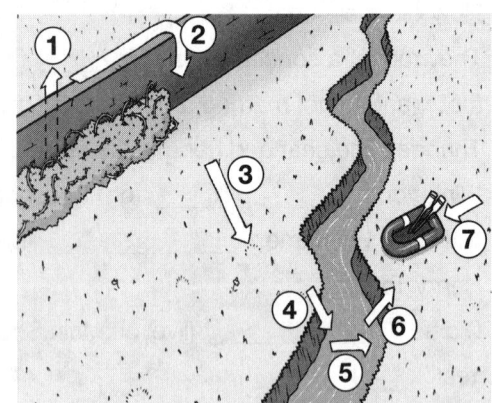

1 _Climb_ up the wall.

2 Walk along the top and then _____ off.

3 _____ across the field.

4 _____ into the river.

5 _____ across to the opposite side.

6 _____ out of the water.

7 Find the boat and _____ it into the water.

Grammar: Past ability: *could* and *was/were able to*

3 ★ Circle the correct answers. Sometimes both choices are correct.

1 Pierre speaks French so he *could* / (was able to) understand the movie.

2 I called Gina ten times before I *could* / *was able to* speak to her.

3 *Could the children* / *Were the children able to* swim when they were babies?

4 My dad *couldn't* / *wasn't able to* go to college.

5 She fell off her bike but she *could* / *was able to* walk home.

6 He *couldn't* / *wasn't able to* dive into the swimming pool because it wasn't deep enough.

7 The weather was very bad but they *could* / *were able to* ski down the mountain.

8 *Could the rescuers* / *Were the rescuers able to* find the lost children?

4 ★★ Complete the sentences with the verbs in the box and the correct form of *could* or *was/ were able to*.

> • do • find • finish • get • ~~read~~ • start • take

1 My little sister is a very good reader. She _could read_ when she was two years old.

2 Anna had listened very carefully in class so she _____ the homework.

3 They had cameras so they _____ a photograph of the shark.

4 Jake stood for the whole trip because he _____ a seat on the train.

5 My father took his computer to a computer technician because he _____ it.

6 I didn't have any money so I _____ on the bus.

7 Simon _____ the marathon but he was too tired to walk home after it.

Consolidation

5 Use the correct form of *could* or *was/were able to* and the verbs in parentheses. Sometimes there is more than one correct answer.

Last winter, Mr. and Mrs. Grange and their two children went for a walk in the snowy mountains near their home in Utah. Unfortunately, the weather changed very quickly. They **1** *couldn't see* (not see) the path and they **2** _____ (not find) their car. They were cold and tired. Luckily, they **3** _____ (make) a snow house to sleep in.

The next morning, they heard rescue helicopters. They ran outside and waved but they **4** _____ _____ (not get) the pilot's attention. There were no trees on the mountain so they **5** _____ (not build) a fire. Their cell phones didn't work so they **6** _____ (not call) for help.

The Granges had to spend a second night on the mountain. They **7** _____ (eat) snow so they weren't dehydrated. However, they **8** _____ (not find) any food so they were very hungry.

On the second morning, Mrs. Grange and her son decided to go look for help. There was a lot of snow but they **9** _____ (walk) down the mountain. After three hours they found a small café. The café owner called the mountain rescue team for them.

The helicopter flew back to the mountain and this time the pilot found Mr. Grange and his daughter. The rescuers **10** _____ (not land) but they **11** _____ (lift) them to safety.

Extra challenge!

6 ★★★ Complete the sentences with the correct form of *used to*, *could*, or *was/were able to* and the verbs in parentheses.

1 In the 1950s, rock bands *didn't use to wear* (not wear) cool clothes. They looked like office workers.

2 Until 1955, people in the U.K. _____ _____ (only watch) BBC television.

3 Before personal stereos, people _____ _____ (not listen) to music everywhere.

4 In 2007, people all over the world _____ _____ (watch) the Live8 concert.

5 Jeans became fashionable in the 1950s. Before then, only workers _____ (wear) them.

6 Before the Internet, musicians _____ _____ (not sell) their own music without a record company.

He had lost his memory.

Vocabulary: Collocations with *lose*

1 ★ **Match the phrases (1–7) with the definitions (a–h). There is one extra definition.**

1 lose interest
2 lose a game
3 lose your memory
4 lose sight of
5 lose your temper
6 lose your way
7 lose weight

a) to forget things
b) to become thinner
c) to become very angry
d) to no longer see something because it has moved
e) to get lost
f) to find a lot of money
g) to become bored
h) to not win a game

2 ★★ **Rewrite the sentences using expressions with *lose*.**

1 Let's go home. I'm bored!
Let's go home. I've lost interest.

2 The Lakers didn't win the game.
_____

3 My parents want to be thinner.
_____

4 She can't remember anything because she hit her head when she fell off her bike.
_____
_____

5 He was worried because he couldn't see the children.
_____
_____

6 Help! I don't know where I am.
_____

7 Theo often used to get very angry when he was younger.
_____
_____

Grammar: Past perfect

3 ★ **Circle the correct answers.**

1 Nobody *heard* / (*had heard*) of the author before we (*studied*) / *had studied* her in English.

2 I *forgot* / *had forgotten* everything in the test even though I *did* / *had done* a lot of studying.

3 Suzy *didn't take* / *hadn't taken* her books home so she *didn't do* / *hadn't done* any homework.

4 The person who *taught* / *had taught* me in elementary school *taught* / *had taught* my mother thirty years before.

5 *Did the teachers move* / *Had the teachers moved* the desks before the test *started* / *had started*?

6 Martin *ran* / *had run* to school because he *slept* / *had slept* late.

7 Iris *did* / *had done* a lot studying because *she got* / *she'd got* bad grades the year before.

8 Before you *went* / *had gone* to school, *did you know* / *had you known* about the test?

4 ★★ **Make sentences. Use the past perfect and the simple past.**

1 the journalist / read about the man / before / she / meet / him
The journalist had read about the man before she met him.

2 Jon / forget / his money / so / he / cannot take / the train

_____

_____

3 Beth / not understand / anything in Spain / because / she / not listen / in her Spanish class

_____

_____

4 Ross / work / for two years / before / he / go / to college

_____

_____

5 someone / steal / Alison's bike / because / she / not lock / it

_____

_____

Consolidation

5 **Complete the article. Use the past perfect or the simple past form of the verbs.**

Last week twenty-five-year-old Jane Mason ¹_disappeared_ (disappear). She ²_____ (leave) her home in Brier to visit her sister in Seattle but she never ³_____ (arrive).

Her sister, Karen Mason, ⁴_____ (go) to meet Jane at the train station. Karen told our reporter, "I ⁵_____ (reach) the station fifteen minutes after the train ⁶_____ (arrive). I ⁷_____ (not be) worried at first because I ⁸_____ (not tell) Jane I was meeting her."

"I waited a day before I called the police. They asked why I ⁹_____ (not call) earlier. I explained that Jane always ¹⁰_____ (change) her plans at the last minute."

Two days later the police found Jane Mason in a hospital in Seattle. She ¹¹_____ (get off) the train at the wrong station and ¹²_____ (get lost). Unfortunately, she ¹³_____ (fall down), hit her head and ¹⁴_____ (lose) her memory.

Luckily, Jane's memory slowly came back and she told the nurses her name. Karen said, "I was so happy when the hospital called!"

Is it fair?

Read

1 ★ Read the article and choose the correct answers.

1 The article is for ____ .

  a) students b) teachers c) parents

2 The article tells you how to ____ .

  a) cheat when you do your homework

  b) do research without cheating

  c) write an essay

2 ★★ Complete the text with the sentences in the box.

- How can you check if the information is correct?
- How do you find what you want?
- This is how you can avoid cheating.
- Here are some tips for successful research.

USING THE INTERNET FOR HOMEWORK AND SCHOOL PROJECTS

It's hard to believe but, before the Internet, students weren't able to look at millions of pages of information in their own homes. They used to do research in libraries. Now, anyone with a computer and an Internet link can simply log on and find what they need.

However, there can be problems using the Internet.
1 _____

There is a lot of information on the Internet.
2 _____

- Choose a popular search engine like Google or Yahoo.
- Think carefully about what you want to find and choose a few important words.
- Type in those key words.
- Restrict your search by putting quotation marks around phrases.
- Bookmark the websites you think are most useful.

Anyone can write a website so don't believe everything you read. 3 _____

- Check the date of the page.
- Cross-check facts in different places.
- Only use pages you trust.
- Learn to see the difference between facts and opinions.

It's easy to cut and paste information but it's dishonest.
4 _____

- *Don't* cut and paste information.
- *Don't* just change one or two words—it's still cheating!
- Use the information to make your own notes.
- Use your notes to write your project.

Remember! Copying information doesn't help you to learn or to pass your tests.

New words

3 ★ Complete the sentences with words from the article.

1 Google and Yahoo are both _search engines_ .

2 To start a search, you type in _____ words.

3 Punctuation marks like these " . . . " are called

_____ _____ .

4 A place on the Internet where you find

information is a _____ .

5 _____ a website you want to visit again.

6 When you copy information from a page, you

_____ and _____ it.

Comprehension

4 ★★ Answer *yes* (Y), *no* (N), or *doesn't say* (DS).

Does the writer think . . .

1 the Internet is useful for students? ☐

2 libraries aren't useful now? ☐

3 young children can't use the Internet? ☐

4 you sometimes get too much information
on the Internet? ☐

5 all websites are correct? ☐

6 websites only have facts in them? ☐

7 you only need to change a few words
before you use the information? ☐

8 you can't learn from copying? ☐

9 teachers don't like the Internet? ☐

Listen

> **Listening strategy: Listening for key words**
> **Remember!** Listen to the words that are stressed.
> These are the key words. They tell the most
> important information.

5 ★ 🎧 7 Listen to the radio news story. Then circle the correct answers.

1 The first speaker is a *teacher / reporter*.

2 The main topic is *the Internet / cheating students*.

3 The story is in the news because

teachers / parents complained.

6 ★★ Listen again and number the sentences in the correct order.

☐ a) After he had read the projects, the teacher
checked on the Internet.

☐ b) Before the summer vacation, the teacher
had given the class a history project.

☐ c) Parents spoke to the principal because their
children had failed.

☐ d) The students gave their work to the teacher.

☐ e) When the teacher found out they had
cheated, he gave them zeros.

☐ f) The teacher spoke to a reporter.

7 ★ 🎧 8 Listen and underline the stressed words.

1 Mr. Kilroy said he had been fair to the students.

2 The students were angry because other people
had used the Internet.

Write

8 ★★ On a piece of paper, write an e-mail to a friend about the story you heard on the radio news.

Tell your friend:

• what happened

• what the teacher did

• what some students and parents did

• what you think about it

What's it made of?

Phrases

1 ★ Complete the conversation with the words and phrases in the box.

> • charity (×2) • donation • in good shape
> • second-hand (×2)

Anna: Do you like this suede jacket?

Mike: Sure, it looks good on you. How much is it?

Anna: It's only $50.

Mike: It's how much? I thought this was a
1 *second-hand* store.

Anna: It is. All the money goes to 2 _____ .
Do you think it's too expensive?

Mike: I don't know. It's 3 _____
for a 4 _____ jacket. And I like
the color.

Anna: Great, then I'll buy it. Are you going to buy
anything?

Mike: I like this hat, but it's pretty expensive.

Anna: But it's for 5 _____ .

Mike: I have an idea. Let's bargain with the
salesperson. We'll ask for a better price for
the jacket and hat together!

Anna: No way! Just think of it as a 6 _____ .

Vocabulary: Materials

2 ★ Label the items with words in the box.

> • cardboard • fur • leather • plastic • silver
> • wooden • woolen

3 ★★ Complete the sentences with the correct materials.

1 I never wear leather or *suede* shoes.

2 In the summer, I wear c_____n clothes.

3 Married people often wear a g_____d ring.

4 For security, the bank has a heavy m_____l
door.

5 In fast-food restaurants, the food is wrapped in
p_____r.

6 Scientists often wear r_____r gloves when
they do experiments.

7 S_____k is a light, soft material. It is
sometimes used to make wedding dresses.

Grammar: Simple present passive

4 ★ Rearrange the words to make simple present passive sentences about a charity book shop.

1 given the books to shop the are .
The books are given to the shop.

2 are on books wooden arranged shelves the .
_____

3 aren't old books sold or dirty .
_____

4 run isn't by the paid staff shop .
_____

5 sold books cheaply the are ?
_____

6 the is the shop in evenings open ?
_____

7 on closed shop is Sundays the .
_____

5 ★★ **Rewrite the sentences in the simple present passive.**

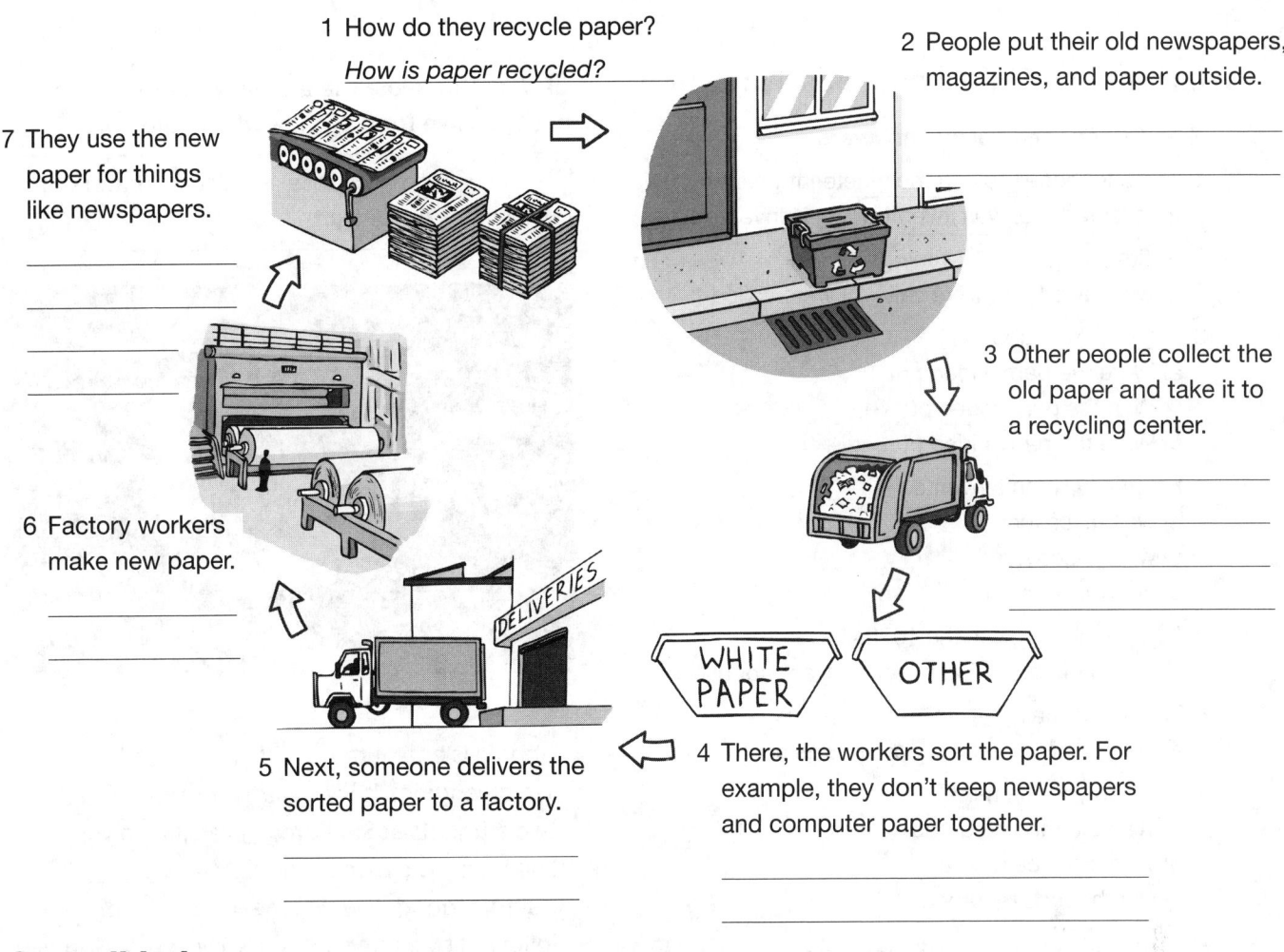

1 How do they recycle paper?

How is paper recycled?

2 People put their old newspapers, magazines, and paper outside.

_____

_____

7 They use the new paper for things like newspapers.

_____

_____

_____

3 Other people collect the old paper and take it to a recycling center.

_____

_____

_____

6 Factory workers make new paper.

_____

_____

5 Next, someone delivers the sorted paper to a factory.

_____

_____

4 There, the workers sort the paper. For example, they don't keep newspapers and computer paper together.

_____

_____

_____

Consolidation

6 **Rosie and Ethan are playing a guessing game. Complete the conversation with the correct form of the simple present passive.**

Ethan: I'm thinking of something. Guess what it is. You can only ask *Yes/No* questions.

Rosie: **1** (it / make of / man-made material?)

Is it made of a man-made material?

Ethan: No, it isn't.

Rosie: **2** (it / make of / natural material?)

_____

Ethan: Yes, it is.

Rosie: **3** (the material / grow / in this country?)

_____

Ethan: Yes, it is.

Rosie: **4** (the material / make / into something else?)

_____

Ethan: Yes, it is.

Rosie: So, it's a natural material and **5** (it / make / into something else.)

_____

Ethan: That's right. I'll give you a clue: the material is made into things sold in clothing stores.

Rosie: **6** (the things / buy / by everyone?)

_____

Ethan: No, **7** (they / not buy / by everyone.)

_____

Rosie: **8** (the things / wear / by young people?)

_____

Ethan: Yes, they are.

Rosie: Are you thinking of T-shirts?

Ethan: Yes, I am!

I was invited to join.

Grammar: Simple past passive

1 ★ Choose the correct answers.

1 The telephone __*b*__ in the nineteenth century.
a) invented   (b) was invented)   c) is invented

2 At first, blogs _____ "weblogs."
a) was called   b) were call   c) were called

3 _____ on YouTube?
a) Were the party video put
b) Was the party video put
c) Were the party video putting

4 Electricity wasn't invented—it _____ .
a) was discover
b) were discovered
c) was discovered

5 Cell phones _____ in the 1970s.
a) weren't used   b) are used   c) are not used

6 The first e-mail _____ in 1971.
a) were sent   b) was send   c) was sent

7 _____ on your camera?
a) Was the race recorded
b) Was the race record
c) Did the race recorded

2 ★★ Rewrite the sentences using the simple past passive.

1 Someone in ancient Egypt made the first paper.
   The first paper was made in ancient Egypt.

2 Did stores give plastic bags to people fifty years ago?

   _____

3 In the past, people didn't make ships from metal.

   _____

4 Nobody knows when people made the first glass.

   _____

5 Someone developed silk-making in China.

   _____

6 Did someone build a simple computer in the nineteenth century?

   _____

   _____

3 ★★ Complete the article with the simple past passive form of the verbs in the box.

• add • build • choose • collect • draw (× 2)
• invent • put • ~~start~~

Google is one of the world's most-used search engines. It [1]*was started* in 1996 by two students at Stanford University. Do you know why the name "Google" [2]_____ ? It's from "googol" which means a number 1 followed by a hundred zeros. The word "Google" [3]_____ to show that they wanted to organize all the information in the world.

In 2004, Google Earth [4]_____ . Google Earth allows you to "fly" to anywhere in the world. It [5]_____ by putting together satellite photographs. In 2006, historic old maps [6]_____ on Google Earth. There is a map of Tokyo that [7]_____ in 1680 and several from North America that [8]_____ in the nineteenth century.

The old maps used on Google Earth [9]_____ by David Rumsey. He has more than 150,000 maps in his collection.

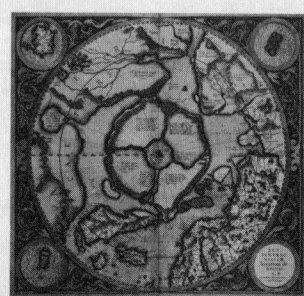

Use your English: Give and react to opinions

4 ★ Are the phrases *giving opinions* (G), *agreeing* (A), or *disagreeing* (D)?

1 Actually, I think you're wrong. `D`
2 I agree. ☐
3 I think . . . ☐
4 I don't think so. ☐
5 I know/see what you mean but . . . ☐
6 I can't stand . . . ☐
7 (I'm afraid/Sorry but) I don't agree ☐
8 I disagree. ☐
9 In my opinion, . . . ☐
10 I think so, too. ☐
11 Yes, you're right/that's true. ☐

5 ★★ Write the conversations.

Conversation 1

A: Tell your friend that you think the Internet is a great place for shopping.

In my opinion, the Internet is a great place for shopping.

B: Agree. _____

Conversation 2

C: Tell your friend you think people spend too much time on Twitter.

_____

_____

D: Disagree. _____

Consolidation

6 Complete the letter with the sentences and phrases in the box.

- All the invitations were sent by text message or e-mail
- I can't stand people who film everything
- In my opinion
- my nephew's wedding suit was bought second-hand
- the photos (and the video) were put on a special wedding website
- ~~the wedding was planned~~
- Where were the tickets bought?

Dear Helen,

My nephew Sam got married last weekend. He met his wife, Claire, on the Internet two years ago. They both spend most of their time online so ¹*the wedding was planned* virtually! ² _____. (³ _____ a real invitation is nicer!) The bride's dress was bought from an online store and ⁴ _____ on eBay.

Some Australian relatives weren't able to come to the wedding so there was a live video link. I thought it was strange that my cousin and his wife were watching on the other side of the world! ⁵ _____ but I think it was a good idea to include everyone. After the wedding, ⁶ _____ my nephew had built.

Sam and Claire flew to Sicily two days after the wedding. ⁷ _____ They weren't sold by a travel agent!

With love,

Alison

Extra challenge!

7 ★★★ Write sentences using the simple present passive or the simple past passive. Use your own ideas.

1 I think the best shoes / make from . . .

I think the best shoes are made from Italian leather.

2 I think last year's best movie / produce in . . .

_____

3 I think the cheapest clothes / sell in . . .

_____

4 I think rubber trees / grow in . . .

_____

5 I think the Internet / invent by . . .

_____

6 I think fake fur / make from . . .

_____

The volcano, which erupted from a cornfield, . . .

Vocabulary: Landscape and environment

1 ★ Write the words in the chart. Some words can go in both columns.

> • coast • forest • hill • island • lake
> • mountain • ocean • river • rock
> • sea • tree • valley • waterfall

Land	Water
coast	coast
forest	

2 ★★ Label the diagram.

1 *sea/ocean*
2 _____
3 _____
4 _____
5 _____
6 _____
7 _____
8 _____
9 _____
10 _____
11 _____
12 _____

Grammar: Nonrestrictive adjective clauses: *who, whose, which, where*

3 ★ Put *who, whose, which,* or *where* and commas (,) in the correct places in each sentence.

　　　　　　　which
1 We walked to a river, is near the

　village, and went swimming.

2 Uncle Charlie lives next to the lake took

　us on a boat trip.

3 They sunbathed on a rock they had

　eaten lunch.

4 We spoke to a woman family had lived

　on the island for two hundred years

　about the area.

5 Fifty trees were all very old fell down in

　the storm.

6 My aunt family all hate swimming

　never goes to the beach.

4 ★ Complete the postcard. Write *who, whose, which,* or *where* and the letter of the phrase.

> A) are all over forty
> B) fish are sold during the day
> C) I am writing this postcard
> D) parents work in the hotel
> E) remembered us from last year
> F) sells fantastic ice cream

Hi!
This is a picture of our hotel. The hotel owner,
¹who E , has given us rooms with a view of the ocean.
From our balcony, ² _____ , I can see the people
on the beach. Today, Mom and Dad won't let me go to the
café, ³ _____ , because I've spent too much money.
The other people in the hotel, ⁴ _____ , have
complained about my music! Carla, ⁵ _____ ,
is the only other teenager. This evening, Carla and I are
going to the harbor, ⁶ _____ , for a concert.
Love, David

5 ★★ Complete the sentences with the nonrestrictive adjective clauses (a–e) and the endings (f–j).

1 The lives of Bedouin people, *who live in desert areas, are changing.*

2 The Pacific Ocean, _____

_____

3 The forests of Borneo and Sumatra, _____

_____

4 Brazilian people, _____

_____

5 The top of Mount Kilimanjaro, _____

_____

a) which is between North America and Asia

b) whose first language is Portuguese

c) where orangutangs live in the trees

d) ~~who live in desert areas~~

e) which is the highest mountain in Africa

f) is the world's largest body of water.

g) ~~are changing.~~

h) is covered with snow.

i) can usually learn Spanish easily.

j) are disappearing.

Consolidation

6 Write sentences. Use nonrestrictive adjective clauses.

1 Fraser Island beach / Australia / 90 miles long

Fraser Island beach, which is in Australia, is 90 miles long.

3 Emperor penguins / live in Antarctica / travel 60 miles from the coast to lay their eggs

_____

_____

2 Jeanne Louise Calment / died aged 122 in 1997 / the world's oldest person

_____

_____

4 Jamling Tenzing Norgay / father climbed Everest in 1953 / climbed the mountain in 1996

_____

_____

5 Kenya / children run long distances to school / produces the world's best runners

_____

_____

Climate change

Read

1 ★ Read the article and choose the correct answers.

1 The article is about ____ carbon footprint.
   a) a school's   b) a school reducing its
   c) how to reduce your

2 The school gives money to ____ .
   a) another school   b) other countries
   c) a charity

Many schools are trying to reduce their carbon footprint and one has already become carbon neutral.

Dalton School in Gateshead, which is in England, figured out how much energy it used. They found out how much carbon and other greenhouse gases were produced by the school. For example, teachers and students decided to look at recycling. In the past, they had sent all their garbage to a landfill site. Now, all their old paper is recycled and leftover food is used to make compost for the school gardens.

On a visit to the school, a climate expert told the students that a quart of gas produces the equivalent of six bathtubs full of carbon dioxide. As a result, a big effort was made by the school to reduce its carbon footprint. Now, 60% of students walk to school, 25% ride their bikes, 10% use public transportation, and only 5% travel by car. However, the school still produces almost eight hundred tons of greenhouse gases a year, so the

school now gives about $11.25 to a climate charity for each ton.

The climate charity, which works with lots of schools, sells carbon offsets. The money given by the school is used to pay for tree planting, low-energy light bulbs, and cheaper, more efficient fuels in poorer countries.

Some people say that carbon offsets aren't a good idea. The problem is that rich countries, which use the most carbon, don't really change: They just pay some money and keep doing the same things. Giving money to poorer countries won't solve the problems because it only moves them somewhere else. However, some green charities say that carbon offsetting makes people think about climate change and as a result, they help people in poorer countries.

New words

2 ★★ Match the new words and phrases (1–7) with the definitions (a–g).

1 carbon neutral
2 leftover (food)
3 compost
4 ton
5 carbon offset
6 low-energy
7 efficient

a) a weight equal to about 2,000 pounds
b) not using a lot of electricity
c) putting no more carbon dioxide into the air
d) works well without making a lot of waste
e) something that has not been eaten by the end of a meal
f) material used to feed the earth and plants
g) a donation or action to reduce the production of carbon dioxide

Comprehension

3 ★★ Answer *true* (T), *false* (F), or *don't know* (DK).

1 All schools want to be carbon neutral. ☐

2 Dalton School wanted to reduce its carbon footprint. ☐

3 Dalton School has done one thing to be more environmentally friendly. ☐

4 The school uses coal for heating. ☐

5 The school gives money to a climate charity. ☐

6 Everyone agrees that carbon offsets solve the problem of global warming. ☐

Listen

4 ★★ 🎧 9 **Read the questionnaire. Listen and answer the questions for Michael.**

How green are you?

1 When the weather's cold, what do you do?
a) Wear a sweater.
b) Ask your parents to turn up the heat.

2 What do you do with leftover food?
a) It goes in the garbage can.
b) It is made into compost.

3 When you are the last person to leave a classroom, do you turn off the lights?
a) Of course!
b) No, I don't.

4 How do you get to school?
a) I walk, ride my bike, or take the bus.
b) My mom or dad drives me.

5 What do you do with your old clothes?
a) I throw them away.
b) I recycle them.

6 How many electrical things do you turn on at the same time?
a) I use one thing at a time and turn off the others.
b) I like to have several things on at the same time.

Write

Learning Strategy: Using linking phrases

Remember! Linking phrases help you when you read. They tell you what you are going to read next.

for example, such as

*Some places, **for example**, parts of Africa, have terrible droughts.*

*Hurricanes are becoming more dangerous. **For example**, in New Orleans people drowned after Hurricane Katrina.*

*Some countries, **such as** Bangladesh, already have awful floods.*

as a result, so

*There isn't enough rain. **As a result**, crops fail and sometimes people starve.*

*Sea levels rise, **so** the land is flooded.*

5 ★ **Read the notes about why people in countries like the U.K. and the U.S. have big carbon footprints. Add three ideas to the ideas map.**

6 ★★ **On a piece of paper, write a report explaining why some people have a big carbon footprint. Remember to use different linking phrases.**

Vocabulary: Vacations

1 ★ Match the pictures (1–6) with the words and phrases (a–f).

1

2

3

4

5

6
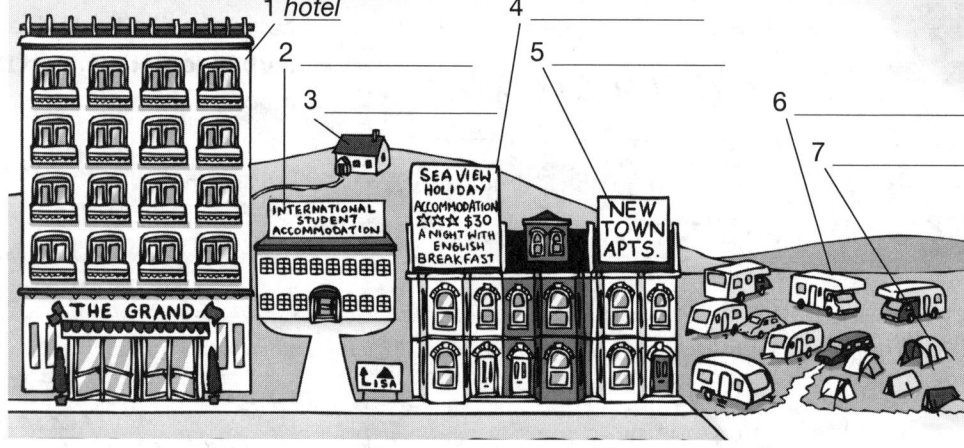

a) camping ___3___

b) climbing _____

c) go to a museum _____

d) mountain biking _____

e) skiing _____

f) windsurfing _____

2 ★ Label the picture with words from the box. There is one extra word.

- apartments
- B & B
- cottage
- hostel
- ~~hotel~~
- motor home
- tent
- villa

1 *hotel*
2 _____
3 _____
4 _____
5 _____
6 _____
7 _____

3 ★★ Complete the postcard.

Dear Justin,

We're having a great time relaxing and doing nothing! Every morning, we ¹<u>go</u> to the <u>beach</u>. It's a two-minute walk from our five-star ² _____ to the beach! We never go swimming. We ³s_____ for 30 minutes before the sun gets too hot. I can see some people playing beach ⁴v_____ but we haven't done that! There are some very nice stores here. After lunch today we may go ⁵ _____ for some presents to take home. We might go ⁶ _____ in Cannes tomorrow, but we don't really enjoy museums and art galleries. We'll probably ⁷ _____ to the _____ as usual!

See you soon.

Love,

Marc, Helena, and the girls

Grammar: *will/won't/may/might* for predictions

4 ★ Complete the information about vacation activities with the phrases in the box.

> • may be • may not have • may see
> • might ask • might not get • might not see

> On the boat trip, you ¹*may see* some dolphins. In bad weather, you ² _____ any good photographs.

> In the National Park you ³ _____ any bears because they sleep in the winter. In Hollywood, you ⁴ _____ lucky and see a famous movie star.

> At the airport, the police ⁵ _____ to look in your bag.

> Large groups staying in the hotel ⁶ _____ rooms on the same floor.

5 ★★ Choose the correct answers.

1 Ted __b__ sleep in a tent! He hates being outdoors.

 a) may (b) won't) c) will

2 Claire's family hasn't decided where to go on vacation. They ___ visit her grandparents in Tacoma or go camping in Vancouver.

 a) might b) won't c) will

3 Our train leaves at 10:30 so ___ meet you at the station at 10:15.

 a) I won't b) I'll c) I may not

4 When the Davies family go on vacation, they ___ travel by train or they ___ go by bus.

 a) will / won't b) may / might c) won't / may not

5 My parents don't have much money right now so we ___ go away on vacation this summer.

 a) will b) may not c) might

6 My family is going to Spain in June. I expect we ___ go swimming every day.

 a) may b) will c) might

7 My older brother, Jon, is sure he ___ save enough money to buy a ticket to Brazil.

 a) will b) may c) might not

6 ★★ Look at the survey about travel in the future. Write sentences about the results.

Survey: Vacations in the future

1 Will people travel to Mars? *100% disagree*

2 Will vacations be more expensive? *50% disagree*

3 Will people try to take greener vacations? *100% agree*

4 Will tourists fly less? *50% agree*

5 Will space travel become common? *100% disagree*

6 Will beach vacations be less popular? *50% agree*

7 Will hotels be smaller? *50% disagree*

8 Will people use the Internet for virtual vacations? *50% agree*

1 (won't) *People won't travel to Mars.* _____

2 (may not/might not) _____

3 (will) _____

4 (may/might) _____

5 (won't) _____

6 (may/might) _____

7 (may not/might not) _____

8 (may/might) _____

Consolidation

7a Complete Karen's vacation plans.

> **Going to:** Colorado
> **Accommodation:** tent
> **Activities:** climbing ? swimming ✗
>   mountain biking ✓

Karen is going to 1 *Colorado* for her vacation. She is going to stay in a 2 _____ . While she is away, she may go 3 _____ , she won't go 4 _____ but she will go 5 _____ .

b Write about Oliver's plans in your notebook.

> **Going to:** Los Angeles
> **Accommodation:** hotel
> **Activities:** swimming ✓ windsurfing ?
>   sightseeing ✗

Phrases

1 ★ Complete the short conversations with the phrases in the box.

| • and stuff • in bad shape • It's supposed to be • No way! • pouring • So what? • test your skills |

Conversation 1

A: Do you want to go on this adventure weekend?

B: I don't know. I'm **1** *in bad shape* .

A: Don't worry, they **2** _____ first and then help you decide which activities to do.

Conversation 2

C: I don't want to go hiking! It's **3** _____ . We'll get wet!

D: **4** _____ A little rain never hurt anyone.

C: Walking in the rain for two hours will be horrible.

    5 _____ fun!

Conversation 3

E: Anyone who wants to try out climbing, meet me in the gym at 4:30.

F: Do we need to bring our helmets **6** _____ ?

E: No, it's OK. We have all the safely equipment in the gym.

Conversation 4

G: I don't want to go windsurfing today. The ocean's too cold.

H: **7** _____ It's 86°F!

Grammar: Conditional clauses with *if/unless*; future time clauses with *when/as soon as*

2 ★ Circle the correct answers.

1 *If* / *Unless* it's pouring rain, we'll sleep outside the tent.

2 You won't be warm enough *if* / *unless* you have a good sleeping bag.

3 *If* / *Unless* we build a fire, we will be able to cook a meal.

4 They won't go camping *if* / *unless* they don't find their tent.

5 We'll save some money *if* / *unless* we walk to the campsite.

6 *If* / *Unless* you wear hiking boots to go hiking, your feet won't hurt.

7 I won't try climbing *if* / *unless* you do, too.

3 ★ Put *when* in the correct places in sentences 1–3. Put *as soon as* in the correct places in sentences 4 and 5.

         when

1 I'll go camping⋀I get a tent.

2 Ben arrives we'll go for a walk.

3 Ursula will go hiking she gets some hiking boots.

4 We're going home the adventure course is over.

5 Ian has eaten lunch he'll explore the countryside.

4 ★ Complete the text with *if, unless, when* or *as soon as.*

Welcome to Green Tree Adventure Vacations.

1 *When* I finish speaking, you'll be shown your rooms. **2** _____ you have paid extra, you will share a room with seven other people. **3** _____ you are with your friends, we will try to put you in the same room.

4 _____ you have unpacked your backpacks, please go to the dining room. You must be at the table at six o'clock **5** _____ you want cold food! **6** _____ you don't eat meat, tell the cook *now*.

7 _____ you finish dinner, there will be a short safety lecture. **8** _____ you have any questions now, I'll see you later.

5 ★★ Write sentences with *if, unless, when,* or *as soon as* and *will*.

1 our parents / agree + we / go to the music festival
If our parents agree, we'll go to the music festival.

2 we / camp + we / get a tent
_____

3 we / not get a tent + we sleep outside
_____

4 I / buy the tickets + they go on sale
_____

5 one of our parents / drive us + we / go by bus
_____

6 my mom / not drive us + we / pay for the gas
_____

7 we / make a decision + we / not go anywhere
_____

8 get to the music festival + we / buy some food
_____

Vocabulary: Negative adjectives with prefixes *un-, in-,* and *im-*

6 ★ Write the adjectives in the chart.

- attractive • comfortable
- dependent • experienced
- formal • friendly • happy
- healthy • interesting • kind
- likely • necessary • patient
- pleasant • popular • possible
- practical • usual

un-	in-	im-
unattractive		

7 ★★ Choose the correct answers.

International Student Hostel:
Travelers' comments

It was ¹ b to sleep! The bed was so ² ___
I was awake all night.
I didn't enjoy staying here. The owner is
very ³ ___. He never smiled or said hello.
The hostel is ⁴ ___ for tourists because it is
a very long walk to any famous sights.
This hostel is ⁵ ___ so it is ⁶ ___ to book a room
before you arrive.
The hostel is in an ⁷ ___ part of town. You are
⁸ ___ to find anywhere nice to visit or eat.

1 a) independent   (b) impossible)   c) unpopular
2 a) uncomfortable   b) impractical   c) informal
3 a) unusual   b) unattractive   c) unfriendly
4 a) unlikely   b) unnecessary   c) impractical
5 a) unpopular   b) unlikely   c) unkind
6 a) informal   b) impossible   c) unnecessary
7 a) unpleasant   b) inexperienced   c) impatient
8 a) impossible   b) unhealthy   c) unlikely

Consolidation

8 ★★ Match the beginnings (1–5) with the endings (a–e).

1 Unless you are independent,
2 Unless he's very good at climbing, it's unlikely
3 You'll be tired if you carry unnecessary
4 If you see something unusual,
5 As soon as it smells unpleasant,

a) wash it.
b) take a photograph.
c) you won't enjoy traveling alone.
d) he'll learn to do it in a day.
e) things on the hike.

Don't forget your camera.

Vocabulary: Phrases in e-mails

1 ★ Rearrange the words to make phrases used in e-mails.

1 from love ,

Love from,

2 while I from you in heard a haven't .

_____

3 back write soon .

_____

4 you soon see .

_____

5 was to great you it hear from .

_____

6 all now for that's .

_____

7 I haven't sooner written sorry .

_____

8 for e-mail your thanks .

_____

9 wishes best,

_____

10 are doing how you ?

_____

2 ★ Number the parts of the e-mail in the correct order.

☐ a) I can't wait to meet you and your family next week. My flight arrives at 3:00 P.M. I'll take the airport bus into the city and meet you at the bus station.

☐ b) That's all for now.

☐ c) Sorry I haven't written for a while but I've been really busy.

☐ d) Best wishes,
Maria

1 e) From: Maria Portillo
To: Eran Snyder
Subject: Next week's visit

☐ f) Hi Fran,

☐ g) Sent: Monday, June 5th 4:46 P.M.

Write

3 ★★ **You are Fran. Reply to Maria's letter.**

- Write the subject and the date.
- Start with *Hi Maria.*
- Thank Maria for her e-mail.
- Explain that you and your mom will meet her at Seattle airport.
- Say that you are looking forward to meeting her.
- End in a friendly way and sign your name.

Use your English: Give reminders / reassurances and make promises / offers

4 ★ **Complete the phrases.**

Conversation 1

A: **1** R*emember* to take your shorts for soccer.

B: **2** D_____ w_____y, I'll remember.

Conversation 2

C: **3** M_____ s_____ you remember your project tomorrow.

D: **4** It's OK, I w_____ f_____ .

Conversation 3

E: **5** D_____ f_____ there's a test on Thursday.

F: **6** I p_____ I won't forget.

Conversation 4

G: **7** W_____ y_____ l_____ m_____ to help you study?

H: Yes, please. **8** T_____ w_____ b_____ g____ .

Conversation 5

L: I'll come to your house, **9** i____ y_____ l____ . You might sleep late.

M: Don't worry, I **10** _____ . I always wake up early.

5 ★★ **Write the conversations.**

Conversation 1

A: Remind your friend you are going to a concert together.

_____

_____

B: Say you haven't forgotten.

_____

A: Offer to pick up the tickets.

_____

B: Agree and say it's a good idea.

_____

Conversation 2

C: Offer to babysit with your friend tomorrow night.

_____

D: Say no and explain that you are going to do your French homework.

_____

_____

C: Tell your friend not to forget the French dictionary.

_____

D: Promise you won't forget.

_____

Consolidation

6 On a piece of paper, write an e-mail to someone in your family who is coming to visit you for your grandfather's birthday.

In your letter:
- offer to meet him or her at the station
- reassure him or her that you will buy the birthday present
- remind him or her to bring their camera

Extra challenge!

7 ★★★ **Complete the sentences so they are true for you.**

1 As soon as I save enough money, I'*ll buy a guitar* .

2 My best friend never remembers _____ .

3 I send e-mails to _____ .

4 When I'm eighteen, I _____ .

5 I'll never go on a _____ vacation.

6 My friends and I might _____ next summer.

7 If I see my friends tonight we might _____

_____ .

8 My teachers often say, "Don't forget _____

_____ ."

Gap years

Read

1 ★ Read the three texts. Where are they from: a blog, a poster, or a book cover?

A _____

B _____

C _____

2 ★ Choose the correct answers.

1 The writer of text A wants you to _____ .

  a) buy the book   b) go on a gap year

2 The writer of text B wants you to _____ .

  a) have a good experience   b) apply for a job

3 The writer of text C wants to _____ .

  a) give advice to other "gappers"

  b) tell their family and friends what they are doing

A

You're young, you've just left school, and you're looking for adventure!

This guidebook gives you practical information and advice on:

- where to go and how to get there
- traveling independently or as part of a group
- working as a volunteer
- places to study
- staying healthy and safe
- earning money
- cheap accommodations

A gap year is for you and this book is for all "gappers"!

B

Work 4 Real
is looking for volunteers.

We organize camping and adventure vacations for disabled teenagers and we need young people to travel with the group and to help with the activities.

Volunteers aren't paid, but you will get free accommodations, all your meals, and travel. We also train all our volunteers, so this is a great opportunity to learn some new skills.

Our destinations include Wales, Spain, Poland, and Italy.

Interested? Phone 020 83763 9372 or visit our website *work4real.org.uk*

C

Day 1

It's 8:30 P.M. and we arrived an hour ago. It's pitch-black so we can't see the mountains. Our room in the hostel is small, but warm and comfortable. We start our jobs in the café tomorrow afternoon. If the weather's good in the morning, we'll go skiing.

Day 2

It's lunchtime and we had a great morning! We got up early and skied for hours. As soon as we finish lunch, we'll walk to town and find the café.

Day 3

It's 10:30 and I just got up. The café where we're working is horrible. It's very formal and the people are very unfriendly. Unless it's better tonight, I'll look for another job.

New words

3 ★★ **Match the new words (1–4) with the definitions (a–d).**

1 guidebook
2 destination
3 pitch-black
4 horrible

a) a place that someone or something is going to
b) very bad or unpleasant
c) a book that gives travel information
d) completely dark, no light

Comprehension

4 ★★ **Answer** *true* **(T),** *false* **(F), or** *don't know* **(DK).**

1 The guidebook is for people traveling with a lot of money. ☐
2 The guidebook tells where you can work. ☐
3 The guidebook is only for travelers on specially arranged trips. ☐
4 Work4Real gives disabled teenagers experience with outdoor activities. ☐
5 Volunteers at Work4Real must have worked with disabled people before. ☐
6 Work4Real adventure vacations are in July and August. ☐
7 The blog writer is traveling with his sister. ☐
8 The blog writer isn't enjoying anything. ☐
9 The blog writer will look for another job if he doesn't enjoy it tonight. ☐

Listen

5 ★ 🎧10 **Listen and choose the correct answers.**

1 Julia and her uncle are talking about her *tests / future*.
2 Julia *is / isn't* going to college next year.
3 Julia *will never / wants to* go on a gap year.
4 *Some / A few* of Julia's friends want to travel when they are older.
5 Her uncle *had / didn't have* a gap between school and college.
6 Her uncle is a *waiter / teacher* now.

6 ★★ **Listen again and number the sentences about Julia's uncle in the correct order.**

☐ a) He became a teacher.
☐ b) He did another term at school.
1 c) He failed some of his classes.
☐ d) He wanted to be a teacher.
☐ e) He was a waiter.
☐ f) He was a volunteer.

Write

Learning Strategy: Using headings to organize text
Remember! When you plan your writing, headings can help you to arrange your ideas. You can include these headings in your outline and in the final draft.

7 ★ **Make notes for these headings.**
Reasons for a gap year
1 *It's a great experience and you learn a lot.*
2 _____
3 _____

Reasons against a gap year
1 *It's a waste of time.*
2 _____
3 _____

Conclusion
Good for people who:
1 *want to have a break between school and work.*
2 _____

Not good for people who:
1 *don't like being away from home.*
2 _____

8 ★★ **On a piece of paper, write an article about whether people should have a gap year or not.**

Gap years: should you go or shouldn't you?
A gap year is a break between school and work or college.

65

He told them to buy some socks.

Grammar: Reported requests and commands

1 ★ Rearrange the words to make reported requests and commands.

1 the to the joke asked explain She journalist .   *She asked the journalist to explain the joke.*

2 told readers spaceships to look for the article .   _____

3 to not told her the *fatsox* story believe the doctor .   _____

4 asked I brother not to trick anyone my .   _____

5 not the people to told travel in UFOs article .   _____

6 joke the explain readers them to asked the .   _____

2 ★★ Write reported requests and commands.

1 Erik: You must read this book about UFOs. (Erik / tell / Alex)
  Alex: Can you lend it to me, please? (Alex / ask / Erik)

  Erik told Alex to read a book about UFOs. Alex asked Erik to lend it to him.

2 Dan: Please drive me to school. (Dan / ask / his mom)
  Mom: Don't be lazy! (mom / tell / Dan)

  _____

3 Teacher: Don't forget your homework. (the teacher / tell / Kelly)
  Kelly: Can you please give me an extra day? (Kelly / ask / the teacher)

  _____

4 Dad: Clean up your bedroom! (Gina's dad / tell / her)
  Gina: Oh, Dad! Can you tell Tessa to do it? (Gina / ask / her dad)

  _____

5 Mom: Don't forget to buy some milk. (Jane's mom / told / her)
  Jane: Can you give me some money, please? (Jane / ask / her)

  _____

Vocabulary: Adjective word order

3 ★ Write the adjectives in the table.

- ~~amazing~~ • ~~Australian~~
- beautiful • big • blue
- brown • cardboard
- Chinese • fantastic
- glass • green • horrible
- Italian • little • long
- metal • new • old
- paper • Polish • red
- Spanish • unsuccessful
- woolen • yellow

opinion	size/age/shape	color	origin	material
amazing			*Australian*	

4 ★ Put the adjectives in parentheses in the correct places in the sentences.

       new
1 I saw an exciting Australian movie. (new)

2 Please don't wear that old brown jacket. (horrible)

3 She bought a beautiful blue silk dress. (Chinese)

4 Did you see that amazing green bird. (big)

5 He always wears a long Italian sweater. (black)

6 We all sat at a long table outside the restaurant. (metal)

5 ★★ Use three adjectives to describe each picture.

- American
- big
- new
- Spanish

1 *a big, new, American* _____ car

- beautiful
- glass
- Italian
- old

2 _____ city

- Chinese
- glass
- paper
- small

3 _____ lantern

- Australian
- big
- brown
- Polish

4 _____ animal

Consolidation

6 Complete the article with the phrases in the box.

> A a famous British actor
> B fascinating short
> C from the cold, dark Antarctic winter
> D horrible, cold weather
> E it was amazing
> F The director of the movie
> ~~G told the audience~~
> H warm, green

TV April Fool's Day jokes

The BBC, a British television company, often makes up a story for April Fool's Day. In 2008, the BBC [1] _G_ that penguins flew north every year to escape [2] _____. The short movie was presented by [3] _____. It showed the penguins flying north from the [4] _____ at the South Pole, over the ocean, and then landing in the trees of the [5] _____, South American rain forest. [6] _____, Professor Alid Loyas, told a British newspaper, "We couldn't believe our eyes, [7] _____." Hundreds of people asked to see the [8] _____ movie again and more than two hundred thousand people watched it on the Internet.

9B She said she couldn't remember.

Grammar: Reported statements

1 ★ Choose the correct answers.

1 Sarah (said) / told that she enjoyed her job.

2 Sal *said / told* Tom to meet him at noon.

3 Bella *said / told* she wanted some money.

4 Mrs. Offord *said / told* the children it was time for bed.

5 Mr. Dawson *said / told* that he would be late.

6 Ian *said / asked* Kathy where she lived.

2 ★★ Write reported statements.

1 "The criminal doesn't have a job."

The police officer *said that the criminal didn't have a job.*

2 "The police are looking for a tall man."

The journalist said _____

_____

3 "I saw two women in a car."

The witness said she _____

_____

4 "The police artist has talked to the witness."

She said _____

_____

5 "The picture will help the police."

He said _____

_____

6 "I can't draw a picture without help from a witness."

The police artist said she _____

_____

4 ★★ Write reported statements with *said* or *told*.

1 the witness / the police what she see

The witness told the police what she had seen.

2 Dan / his parents he want to be a police artist

_____

3 The reporter / it be a serious crime

_____

3 ★★ Complete the interview. Use the text to help you.

The witness said her name was Anna Lewis and she lived on Third Street. She told the reporter that she had gotten home at six o'clock and had started to cook dinner.

Next, the witness said that she had heard a loud bang and that she hadn't known what it was. She had looked out of the window, but she couldn't describe the scene because it had been too horrible.

She told him that she hadn't been able to go home and that she would stay with her sister for the night.

Witness: My 1 *name's* Anna Lewis and I 2 _____ Third Street.

Reporter: What time did you get home this evening?

Witness: 3 _____ at six o'clock and I started to cook dinner.

Reporter: What happened next?

Witness: I 4 _____ and I 5 _____ it was. I 6 _____ the window.

Reporter: Tell me what you saw, please.

Witness: I 7 _____ the scene because 8 _____ .

Reporter: Have you been able to go back to your house?

Witness: No. I 9 _____ so I 10 _____ for the night.

4 The witness / the criminal have a tattoo

_____

5 The police / it be a practical joke, not a crime

_____

6 The woman / she make three phone calls

_____

Vocabulary: Appearance

5 ★ Label the police "Wanted" poster with the words in the box.

- bald • bangs • in his sixties • long curly beard
- middle-aged • mustache • overweight
- ponytail • scar • skinny • tattoo • thin face

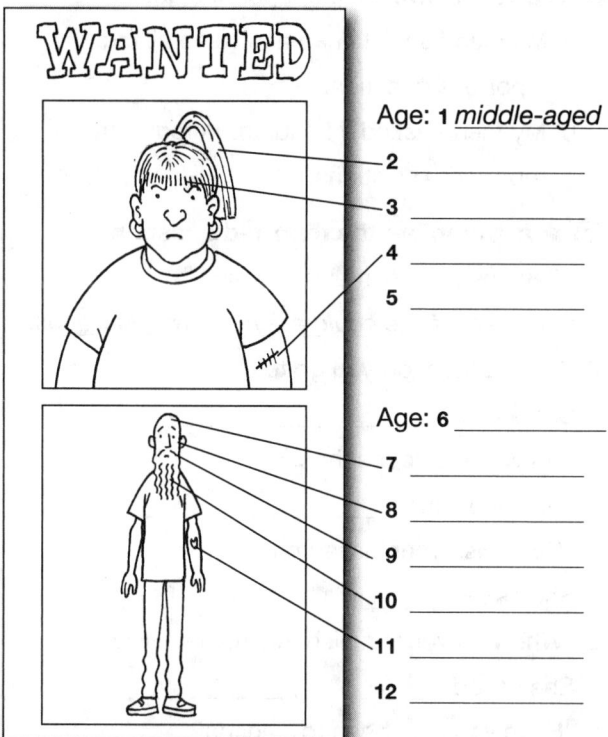

Age: **1** *middle-aged*

2 _____

3 _____

4 _____

5 _____

Age: **6** _____

7 _____

8 _____

9 _____

10 _____

11 _____

12 _____

6 ★★ Complete the descriptions of the people in the police "Missing" posters.

Michael Kenton is in his **1** t*wenties*. He is **2** g_____-l_____ and he wears **3** g_____. He has **4** s_____ **5** d_____ hair and he has a small **6** s_____ on his face.

Paris Clark is an attractive **7** y_____ woman who is nineteen years old. She is **8** t_____ with a **9** p_____ **10** r_____ face and **11** l_____ ears. She has long **12** w_____ hair.

Consolidation

7 Choose the correct answers.

Police artist: I've spoken to your wife. Now I'll ask you the same questions, Mr. Jones. What did the robber look like?

Mr. Jones: He wasn't special or unusual. He was **1** _b_ .

Police artist: That's interesting. Your wife said she thought he was very **2** ____ and that he had lovely dark eyes. What's his build? Was he fat? Thin?

Mr. Jones: He was of medium **3** ____ , he wasn't fat or thin.

Police artist: Your wife told me he was **4** ____ . He looked like an athlete. OK, I'll try another question: How old do you think he was?

Mr. Jones: He's **5** ____-aged, about forty. What did my wife say?

Police artist: She gave a very different answer. She said he was **6** ____ , in his twenties. Your wife told me that he was very **7** ____ — about six feet. Do you agree with her?

Mr. Jones: No, I don't. He was **8** ____ , only about five and a half feet.

Police artist: So, you saw an ordinary, middle-aged man. Your wife saw a tall, dark, handsome young man. Did you see the same person?

1 a) ugly　　　　b) ordinary-looking　　c) good-looking

2 a) handsome　　b) pretty　　　　　　c) beautiful

3 a) build　　　　b) height　　　　　　c) length

4 a) skinny　　　b) well-built　　　　c) overweight

5 a) ordinary　　b) middle　　　　　　c) medium

6 a) young　　　b) very old　　　　　c) teenage

7 a) long　　　　b) slim　　　　　　c) tall

8 a) short　　　　b) fat　　　　　　　c) large

She asked how old I was.

Phrases

1a ★ **Complete the phrases.**

1 I *guess* *so*

2 I____'s s____

3 t____ s____ of t_____

b ★ **Then complete the short conversations.**

Conversation 1

A: Tom, can you help me in the yard today?

B: Yes, *I guess so* . I'm not doing anything.

Conversation 2

C: You were on the phone for an hour. What were you talking about?

D: _____ , I told him about last night's game . . . he said he'd enjoyed his party . . . and I asked him about the math homework.

Conversation 3

E: What are you going to do over the summer?

F: I'm going to go swimming, see my friends, watch some DVDs—_____ , nothing very exciting.

Grammar: Reported questions

2 ★ **Circle the correct answers.**

1 "Do you like pasta?"

  a) She asked if I liked pasta.

  b) She asked if I liked pasta?

2 "How often do you play football?"

  a) He asked how often do I play football.

  b) He asked how often I played football.

3 "Why are soccer shirts so expensive?"

  a) My mom asked me why were soccer shirts so expensive.

  b) My mom asked me why soccer shirts were so expensive.

4 "Has fame changed you?"

  a) She wanted to know if fame had changed me.

  b) She asked if fame had changed me?

5 "Can we go to the game?"

  a) The boys asked if could they go to the game.

  b) The boys asked if they could go to the game.

6 "Did you answer all the reporter's questions?"

  a) My friend said if I had answered all the reporter's questions.

  b) My friend asked if I had answered all the reporter's questions.

3 ★★ **Complete the reported questions.**

1 "Can I ask you some questions?"

She asked *if she could ask me some questions.*

2 "What school do you go to?"

She asked _____

3 "Do you like your school?"

Then she asked _____

4 "Can I visit your classroom?"

She asked _____

5 "Who was your English teacher last year?"

She asked _____

6 "Have you ever been to Canada?"

She asked _____

7 "Will you study English next year?"

She asked _____

Use your English: Speak on the phone

4 ★ **Complete the telephone conversations with words and phrases from the box. There are two extra words or phrases.**

> • Could I speak to • Hello. • I'm sorry but
> • Is / there • It's • Just a minute • May I
> • speaking • take a message • This is

Conversation 1

A: 1 *Hello.*

B: 2 _____ Emily. 3 _____ speak to Robin, please?

A: 4 _____ . I'll get her.

Conversation 2

D: Hi. **5** _____ Jake. **6** _____

Sarah, please?

C: **7** _____ she's out. Can I **8** _____ ?

D: No, thanks. I'll send her a text.

5 ★★ Write the telephone conversations. Use different phrases.

Conversation 1

A: Answer the phone.

_Hello?_____

B: Ask to speak to Joanna.

_____

A: Ask the person to wait while you get Joanna.

_____

B: Say thank you.

_____

Conversation 2

C: Answer the phone.

_____

D: Say who you are and ask to speak to your friend.

_____

C: Say he or she's at the library. Offer to take a message.

_____

D: Say you want to work together on a history project.

_____

C: Promise to tell him or her and say good-bye.

_____

D: Say thank you and good-bye.

_____

Consolidation

6a Complete the conversations with the responses in the box.

- We're not sure. We'll decide later.
- That's a good idea. I know Adam wants to see it, too.
- Sure. Can you tell him I'll meet him outside the movie theater at 7:30?
- ~~Hi Alice, it's Ethan. Can I speak to Adam, please?~~

Alice: Hello. Alice speaking.

Ethan: **1** _Hi Alice, it's Ethan. Can I speak to Adam, please?_

Alice: I'm sorry but he's out. Can I take a message?

Ethan: **2** _____

Alice: OK. What are you going to see?

Ethan: **3** _____

Alice: Diana and I are going to see that new 3D movie. Do you want to come with us?

Ethan: **4** _____

Alice: Great! We'll come with Adam. We'll meet you under the clock. Bye!

b Complete what Alice says when she reports the conversation to her brother, Adam.

Ethan called. He said **1** _he would meet_ you outside the theater at 7:30. I asked

2 _____ going to see. He said you

3 _____ and that **4** _____

later. I explained that Diana and I **5** _____

the new 3D movie and asked if you two **6** _____

_____ . Ethan said **7** _____ because

he **8** _____ you _____ it,

too. We've agreed we'll all go together. I said we

9 _____ him under the clock.

Extra challenge!

7 ★★★ Complete the sentences so they are true for you.

1 Last weekend I asked my parents if _I could sleep_
  at my friend's house.

2 Our teacher asked the class what _____

  _____

3 My English teacher told me to _____

  _____

4 My friend called and asked me to _____

  _____

5 The hairdresser asked me if _____

  _____

6 I told my parents I _____

  _____ when I was older.

Is cheating OK?

Read

1 ★ Read the conversation and the text. Then answer *true* **(T) or** *false* **(F).**

1 Danny invites Charlie to watch a DVD. ☐

2 The movie is about a television show. ☐

3 The makers of the television show were honest. ☐

Danny: Hello?

Charlie: Hi, Danny? It's Charlie. Do you want to come over and watch a DVD?

Danny: What is it?

Charlie: *Quiz Show.*

Danny: I've never heard of it. What's it about?

Charlie: I don't really know but my sister told me that she really enjoyed it.

Danny: I guess so, I'm not doing much. I'll see you later. Bye.

Charlie: Great, see you later.

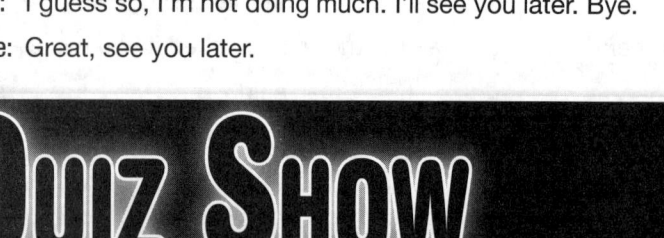

QUIZ SHOW

1995

130 mins

Starring Ralph Fiennes and John Turturro

This excellent movie is based on real events from the 1950s. In the U.S., television game shows were very popular and the show *Twenty One* had a problem: a rather boring, ordinary-looking man named Herbert Stempel was winning every week. He was brainy but the audience didn't think he was attractive enough. The people who made the show wanted a more handsome winner so they gave the answers to another player: a good-looking college professor named Charles Van Doren. Week after week, Van Doren answered difficult questions and won more than $100,000 in prize money. The show's makers were delighted with their success but Van Doren felt very guilty. His winning streak ended when he decided to lose to another player.

Rumors started that the show's makers and Van Doren were cheating and there was a U.S. government investigation. Van Doren told the government that he had cheated on the game show and that the show's makers had helped him.

"A fascinating movie with great actors about the world's first TV game show scandal."
The Washington Post

New words

2 ★★ **Match the new words and phrases (1–7) with the definitions (a–g).**

1 event
2 game show
3 professor
4 guilty
5 winning streak
6 rumor
7 scandal

a) something which is famous because it shocked people
b) a college teacher
c) something that happens which is important, interesting or unusual
d) information or a story that is passed between people which may or may not be true
e) a television show in which people play games or answer questions to win prizes
f) a period of time when you win every game or competition
g) feeling bad because you have done something wrong

Comprehension

3 ★★ **Choose the correct answers.**

1 Danny and Charlie ____ the movie.
  a) aren't going to watch
  b) don't know much about
  c) know a lot about

2 The movie *Quiz Show* was made in ____ .
  a) the 1950s b) the 1970s c) the 1990s

3 Herbert Stempel lost the game because ____ .
  a) he was handsome b) he wasn't smart
  c) someone cheated

4 In the end, Van Doren ____ .
  a) donated his prize money to charity
  b) was angry when he lost
  c) wanted someone else to win

5 At the time, ____ talking about cheating on the show.
  a) nobody was b) some people were
  c) someone was

6 Van Doren said ____ .
  a) "The show's makers helped me cheat."
  b) "I didn't want to cheat."
  c) "The show's makers didn't know I cheated."

Listen

> **Listening tip: Be patient**
>
> If you don't understand everything, don't worry. Listen for key words, and wait for the next sentence.

4 ★ 🎧 11 **Listen and circle the correct answers.**

Part 1

1 *Lily / Andy* is worried about Claire.

Part 2

2 Bella *is / isn't* worried about Claire.

Part 3

3 The principal *believes / doesn't believe* her.

5 ★★ **Listen again. Then answer** *true* **(T) or** *false* **(F).**

Part 1

1 Lily asked Andy not to repeat what she said. ☐
2 Andy asked where Claire went. ☐

Part 2

3 Andy asked if Bella had heard the bad news. ☐
4 Bella said she had seen Claire in science. ☐
5 Andy said Claire had gone to Portland. ☐

Part 3

6 Mrs. Harris said she was too busy to talk to Bella. ☐
7 Mrs. Harris said she had spoken to Claire. ☐
8 Mrs. Harris is pleased that there is a rumor. ☐

Write

6a ★ **Think of a movie you have enjoyed and write some notes in your notebook.**

Title: _____
Actors: _____
The story: _____

b ★★ **On a piece of paper, use your notes to write the DVD cover.**

Grammar: Conditional: *if* clause + *would*

1 ★ Choose the correct answer.

1 If I lost my friend's phone, _b_ tell her.

   a) I'll   (b) I'd   c) I won't

2 If I ___ a noise at night, I'd wake up my parents.

   a) heard   b) hear   c) am hearing

3 Where would you go if you ___ travel anywhere?

   a) could   b) can   c) don't

4 If a friend ___ some gossip about me,
   I'd be angry.

   a) repeats   b) repeating   c) repeated

5 I'd learn Italian if ___ English.

   a) I'm not studying

   b) I wasn't studying

   c) I don't studying

6 If I found a gold ring in the street, I ___ keep it.

   a) don't   b) won't   c) wouldn't

**2 ★★ Complete the conditional sentences
with the correct form of the verbs in the box.
Use *would* where necessary.**

> • ask • be • do • not be surprised
> • not know • ~~tell~~ • want

1 If a salesperson gave me too much change,
   I_'d tell_ him or her.

2 If my parents _____ to move to another
   city, I'd be excited.

3 I _____ if I didn't get a good grade on
   the English test.

4 If a friend _____ angry with you, how
   would you feel?

5 What _____ you _____ if someone
   offered you some money to do their homework?

6 If someone in the street _____ you for
   some money, would you give them any?

7 If you _____ how to do this exercise,
   would you ask a friend for help?

**3 ★★ Read the problem. Then write
conditional sentences.**

> Help! I have a problem! My sixteen-year-old
> brother has some new friends and I don't like
> them. They stay out late at night and they are
> always in trouble at school. What can I do?
> Daisy

1 my brother / have / some bad friends / I / tell /
   our parents

   *If my brother had some bad friends, I'd tell our
   parents.*

2 I / speak / to my brother / I / be / worried
   about him

   _____

   _____

3 my brother / be / sixteen / I / not do anything

   _____

   _____

4 I / have / a problem like yours / I / ask / my
   friends for help

   _____

   _____

5 you / introduce / him to some other people /
   he not have time for his new "friends"

   _____

   _____

6 how / you / feel / he / choose / your friends?

   _____

   _____

Vocabulary: *-ed* and *-ing* adjectives

4 ★ Circle the correct answers.

1 I think it's (annoying)/ *annoyed* when people
   drop paper in the street.

2 The band's performance was *disappointing* /
   disappointed.

3 Do you get *exciting / excited* before a party?

4 It was a *shocking / shocked* crime.

5 We were all *surprising / surprised* when our math and English teachers got married.

6 I was *interesting / interested* in the subject so I listened carefully.

7 They were all *shocking / shocked* when they heard about the accident.

8 Ben's parents were *disappointing / disappointed* when they saw his report card.

5 ★★ Complete the e-mail with the correct adjective form of the verbs in the box. There may be more than one possible answer.

* amaze • annoy • bore • embarrass • excite
* frighten • ~~tire~~

From: **Henry**

To: **Danny**

Hi Danny!

It's great here in Australia! We were all very ¹*tired* after the twenty-hour flight so we relaxed and didn't do anything ² _____ for the first few days.

Yesterday we all climbed the Sydney Harbor Bridge. I loved it. We climbed high above the water and it was really ³ _____ . At night we went to the Sydney Opera House—I was very ⁴ _____ so I fell asleep.

My uncle and his wife live in an ⁵ _____ house on the beach. I was ⁶ _____ when I woke up on the first day and saw the ocean! I've been swimming every day but Joanne wouldn't go for three days because I told her there were lots of sharks. She finally told Mom she was ⁷ _____ of sharks. Mom was really ⁸ _____ with me and sent me to my bedroom for an hour. It was so ⁹ _____ !

I had a ¹⁰ _____ experience yesterday. I woke up and there was a very BIG spider on my bed! I screamed which was ¹¹ _____ . But I was more ¹² _____ when Joanne (six years old) carried the spider into the yard for me.

See you soon,

Henry

Consolidation

6 Write questions for a quiz. Use the conditional.

What would *you* do . . .?

1 you / see / friend cheating on a test / what / you / do?

a) tell the teacher   b) do nothing

If you saw a friend cheating on a test, what would you do?

a) *I'd tell the teacher.*   b) *I'd do nothing.*

2 what / you / do / found / $50 / on the classroom floor?

a) give it to the school secretary   b) keep it

a) _____

b) _____

3 you / be / worried / about your sister's choice of friends / you / tell your parents?

a) yes   b) no

a) _____

b) _____

4 you / tell your friend / her new clothes / be / embarrassing?

a) yes   b) no

a) _____

b) _____

5 what / you / do / win a lot of money?

a) share it with my family and friends   b) keep it all

a) _____

b) _____

6 your friend / tell / you some exciting gossip / who / you / tell?

a) no one   b) everyone

a) _____

b) _____

I wish they paid me more.

Vocabulary: Phrasal verbs

1 ★ Choose the correct phrasal verbs.

1 Can you *find out* / *run out* how much a store manager earns?

2 *Turn on!* / *Look out!* There's a car coming.

3 Would you *give up* / *cheer up* chocolate for a month?

4 Please *turn on* / *go on* with your story, it's very interesting.

5 *Get up* / *Give up* or you'll be late for school.

2 ★★ Complete the sentences with the correct form of the phrasal verbs in the box.

> • to cheer up • to find out • to get up
> • to run out of • to turn on

1 I was shocked when I *found out* how rich some people are.

2 Can you _____ the television, please?

3 I couldn't have toast this morning because we _____ bread.

4 We _____ at 4:30 in the morning to go to the airport!

5 You look unhappy. _____ !

Grammar: *I wish* with simple past

3 ★ Choose the correct verbs.

1 I'm a hairdresser and I wish I _*b*_ more money.
   a) earns   b) earned
   c) has earns

2 My rich parents ___ me lots of presents but I wish they ___ more time with me.
   a) buy / spent   b) bought / spend
   c) bought / spent

3 My hardworking aunt said, "I wish I ___ spend more time with my children."
   a) can   b) couldn't
   c) could

4 I wish tests ___ so stressful.
   a) aren't   b) wasn't
   c) weren't

5 I wish my dad ___ a new laptop and ___ me his old one.
   a) will buy / gave   b) buys / would give
   c) would buy / give

6 We're going to the beach today. I wish ___ sunny.
   a) it was   b) it's   c) it's going to be

4 ★★ Write sentences using *I wish* and the ideas in the box.

> • the computer / will break down   • I / can go home
> • nobody / call for twenty-four hours   • I / be climbing out of the building
> • I / have a lot of money   • I / be a rock star

1 I wish *nobody would call for twenty-four hours.*

2 I wish _____

3 I wish _____

4 I wish _____

5 I wish _____

6 I wish _____

Consolidation

5 Write sentences. Use *I wish* with the simple past form of the phrasal verbs.

1 you / get up / earlier

I wish you got up earlier.

2 we / not run out of / milk every day

_____

3 my sons / get along / like your daughters

_____

4 they / turn on / the heat

_____

Extra challenge!

6 ★★★ Complete the sentences so they are true for you.

1 If the receptionist at the doctor's office told me to

hold on, I'd *wait until she called my name* .

2 I'd turn on _____

if I wanted to know what was in the news.

3 I'd get up early on the weekends if _____

_____ .

4 I'd give up _____

if my friends did, too.

5 If _____ ,

it would cheer me up.

6 If I found out a friend was cheating, I'd _____

_____ .

7 I wish _____ .

8 I wish I didn't have to _____

_____ .

Vocabulary: Types of TV shows

1 ★ Match the pictures (1–6) with the TV shows (a–g). There is one extra show type.

a) cartoon

b) talk show

c) cooking show

d) gardening show

e) game show

f) sports

g) ~~the news~~

 1 g
 2
 3
 4
 5
 6

2 ★★ Complete the TV guide with show types from the box. There is one extra type.

> • talk show • documentary • movie • sports • music show • pop star contest
> • reality show • sitcom (situational comedy) • ~~soap opera~~

This week's best ...

1 _soap opera_: _Bliss Apartments_ continues to be very silly but fantastically dramatic. The four families in the apartments plan a party. Will Ella learn that Henry is her brother? Will the Wilsons get the money from their rich grandmother? Who is Marcia's mysterious visitor?

2 _____: _Eighteen and Leaving Home_. The fourth show in this fascinating factual series which started eighteen years ago. The show makers have followed the teens and their families from birth, at six, twelve, and now at eighteen years old as they prepare to leave home.

3 _____: _Ollie Zewack and Friends_. Stay up late to watch live performances from the nation's best jazz musicians.

4 _____: This is week four of _Hidden Camera House_ and there are only six people left. The camera is on twenty-four hours a day, seven days a week, so a lot of it is really boring. But sometimes it's _very_ interesting!

5 _____: _Michaela Parker Interviews_. A mix of informal conversations and in-depth interviews. This week her guests are Hollywood legend John Travolta and singer Beyoncé.

6 _____: _The Fanshaw Family_. After five years, this is still the funniest show on TV with the best jokes. Erika and Bob take the children to the zoo where young Albert falls into the penguins' pool.

7 _____: _The Golden Compass_ which won the Oscar for Best Visual Effects in 2008. Get a pizza, relax, and enjoy it with your friends.

8 _____: This is the final week of _I Wish I Was Famous_ so remember to vote for your favorite. The three singers left are Tyron Smith, Georgia Kennedy, and Leo Perkins. They're all good but only one person will win on Saturday night.

Phrases

3 ★ Complete the phrases.

1 Can you k_____ an e_____ on the time, please? I want to watch the game at eight o'clock.

2 C_____ d_____ and tell me why you are arguing.

3 You can watch this show tomorrow. Y_____ k_____ , it's on again at six o'clock tomorrow night.

4 ★★ **Complete the conversation with the correct phrases.**

Kate: Mom, Pete won't let me watch my favorite sitcom.

Mom: You two have this disagreement every night.

Pete: Kate started it! I was watching the news and she changed the channel!

Mom: Did you, Kate?

Kate: Yes, but he wasn't watching the news! **1** _____ , he was doing it to be annoying!

Pete: That's not true! I'm very interested and I like to **2** _____ what's happening in the world.

Mom: Stop shouting both of you. Go to your bedrooms and **3** _____ .

Kate: Mom! But we always watch TV at night.

Use your English: Make suggestions, respond, and express preferences

5 ★ **Rearrange the words to make sentences. Then decide if the sentence is *making a suggestion* (S), *giving a response* (R), or *expressing a preference* (P).**

1 watch prefer a pop star contest to I'd .

   I'd prefer to watch a pop star contest. (P)

2 don't I want that really .

   _____

3 watch could a show we reality .

   _____

4 a cartoon I'd not watch rather .

   _____

5 good that sounds yes , .

   _____

6 watch let's game a show .

   _____

7 watch we should soccer ?

   _____

6 ★ **Number the sentences in the correct order to make conversations.**

Conversation 1

☐ a) I'm not crazy about reality shows. I'd prefer to watch a comedy.

☐ b) OK, that sounds good.

☐ c) Should we watch a movie on DVD?

[1] d) Why don't we watch a reality show?

Conversation 2

☐ a) Yes, that sounds good. I love live concerts.

☐ b) No, not really. I never find them funny.

☐ c) We could watch a music show.

☐ d) Do you want to watch a sitcom?

Conversation 3

☐ a) How about going out?

☐ b) I'd prefer not to, it's boring!

☐ c) Do you want to watch the news?

☐ d) Yes, that sounds good. Let's go to the park.

Consolidation

7 **Replace the words in parentheses with a type of TV show.**

1 Should we watch a (show where the guests answer lots of questions and try to win prizes)?

   Should we watch a game show?

2 Do you want to watch a (show with lots of different guests who talk about their books, movies, and lives)?

   _____

3 We could watch a (children's show with moving pictures made from lots of drawings).

   _____

4 I'd rather not watch a (show about growing flowers, fruit, and vegetables).

   _____

5 We'd prefer to watch a (story which is on TV several times a week and follows the lives of a group of people).

   _____

American summer camps

Read

1a ★ Guess what each camp does.

1	Sports International		performing arts camp
2	West Country Adventure Camp	is a / an	sports camp
3	Math 'n' Fun		outdoor activity camp
4	Campfit		weight loss camp
5	Stage Camp		academic camp

b ★ Now read the ads and check your ideas.

2 ★★ Complete the ads (1–5) with the sentences and phrases (a–e).

a) a full range of fun activities

b) However, there are no TVs, DVDs, or video games

c) Although this is a sleep-away camp

d) Learn to surf, swim, and climb

e) to swimming and gymnastics

Comprehension

3 ★★ At which camp can you:

a) lose weight? _____

b) learn to do hip-hop? _____

c) sleep outside? _____

d) do academic things? _____

e) not eat chips or chocolate? _____

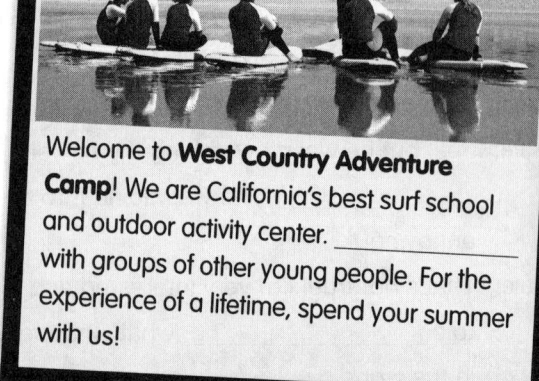

② Welcome to **West Country Adventure Camp!** We are California's best surf school and outdoor activity center. _____ with groups of other young people. For the experience of a lifetime, spend your summer with us!

③ **Math 'n' Fun Camp** welcomes students aged thirteen to sixteen years old. Mornings are spent working on fascinating math problems and, in the afternoons, there is _____ including chess, crosswords, Scrabble, hiking, performing arts, and canoeing.

④ *Campfit* is a camp where our young residents learn to eat properly, enjoy regular exercise, and make new friends. Campfit is fun and friendly—and at the end of a month you'll look fantastic! A typical day includes swimming, dancing, walking—and, of course, healthy meals. _____ !

⑤ **Stage Camp** gives you a full range of performing arts activities from traditional to modern, including music, dancing, and acting. Our students are aged twelve to seventeen years old. _____, we will allow some day campers if we have space. At the end of the three-week course, everyone performs in a big show. Check out our website for photos of last year's happy performers!

① **Sports International** is a day camp for students aged seven to eleven years old. We specialize in all sports from basketball and soccer _____. Students who attend can improve their skills and learn new sports in a safe, encouraging environment.

Listen

4 ★ 🎧(12) **Listen to Alice and her friend, Andy, talking on Skype. Which camp did John go to?**

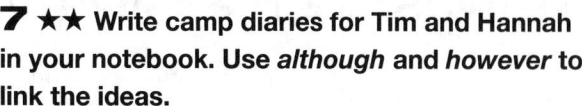

• Campfit

• Math 'n' Fun Camp

• West Country Adventure Camp

5 ★★ **Listen again and choose the correct answers.**

1 Andy *enjoyed / didn't liked* camp.

2 *Alice / Andy* doesn't like surfing very much.

3 Andy took *a lot of / a few* photographs.

4 Alice *is / isn't* interested in his photographs.

5 Alice *went / didn't go* away on vacation this year.

Write

Learning Strategy: Using linking words

Remember! We often link contrasting ideas with *although* or *however*. *Although* links two clauses to make one sentence. *However*, followed by a comma, introduces the new idea in a second sentence.

***Although** there are some day camps, most of the camps are residential.*

*There are some day camps. **However**, most of the camps are residential.*

---

6 ★ **Link the pairs of sentences with *although* and *however*.**

1 It was sunny. Tom stayed indoors.

   Although it was sunny, Tom stayed indoors.

   It was sunny. However, Tom stayed indoors.

2 The campsite was terrible. The children had fun.

   _____

   _____

   _____

3 The ocean was very cold. Cathy and Steve went swimming every day.

   _____

   _____

   _____

7 ★★ **Write camp diaries for Tim and Hannah in your notebook. Use *although* and *however* to link the ideas.**

Tim's camp diary

Having fun in the rain! (although)

Boring food but I'm very hungry! (however)

They're weird but they're my new friends! (although)

Although it's raining, I'm having fun . . .

Hannah's camp diary

The weather is fantastic but I miss you all! (although)

Small but scary! (however)

They're nice but I don't really get along with them. (however)

Crime

11

Vocabulary: Crime

1 ★ Match the pictures (1–6) with the types of criminal (a–f).

a) bank robber d) pickpocket

b) burglar   e) shoplifter

c) mugger   f) vandal

2 ★ Choose the correct answers.

1 The burglar __a__ the building at midnight.

 a) broke into b) caught c) committed

2 The robbers ___ three paintings from the gallery.

 a) burgled b) stole c) mugged

3 My brother's cell phone was ___ .

 a) mugged b) vandalized c) stolen

4 The police haven't ___ anyone yet for yesterday's bank robbery.

 a) catch b) broken c) arrested

5 The graffiti artist ___ a small fine.

 a) went b) paid c) drew

3 ★★ Complete each text with a noun (a–e) and the correct form of a verb (f–j). One verb is used twice.

a) burglar   f) arrest

b) pickpockets g) catch

c) robber   h) draw

d) shoplifters i) steal

e) vandal

1 Earlier today police _arrested_ Mr. James Lewis at his mother's home in Bellevue. Mr. Lewis, a professional _robber_, is wanted for five bank robberies in the Seattle area.

2 The Novak family was surprised by a _____ who broke into their home while they were eating lunch. Dan Novak, 17, _____ the man and sat on him until the police arrived.

3 Nell Hancock, the young graffiti artist who _____ a picture of the governor on a bridge in Seattle, has been fined $100. As Ms. Hancock left the court she told us, "I'm an artist, not a _____."

4 Cotes Supermarket has reported that _____ took more than five hundred things from the store last year. The store manager said that the thieves _____ bread, eggs, and milk as well as more expensive things like meat.

5 Police are warning fans that _____ will be in the crowd at today's concert. "These criminals want to _____ phones and money. Watch out!"

Grammar: *so* + adjective . . . (*that*) . . .; *such* (*a/an*) + adjective + noun (*that*) . . .

4 ★ **Choose the correct answers.**

1 The police were *so*/*such* quick that they arrived before the robbers left.

2 Tom was *so*/*such* a helpful boy that he showed the burglars where his parents kept their money.

3 It was *so*/*such* a hot night that no one closed their windows and there were a lot of robberies.

4 The graffiti artists were *so*/*such* good that no one wanted to cover their pieces.

5 The Rembrandts were *so*/*such* famous paintings the art thieves couldn't sell them.

6 The victim was *so*/*such* angry she hit the mugger with her bag.

7 The news was *so*/*such* frightening that I locked all the doors and windows.

8 She was *so*/*such* a skilled pickpocket that nobody ever felt her take their money.

9 The burglar was *so*/*such* stupid that she left her cell phone in the house.

5 ★★ **Join the sentences with *so* or *such*.**

1 The bank robbers drove a fast car. The police couldn't catch them.

The bank robbers drove such a fast car that the police couldn't catch them.

2 He was a bad pickpocket. He never got anything.

_____

_____

3 She's dishonest. She steals from her own grandmother.

_____

_____

4 The damage to the building was bad. The vandals were sent to prison.

_____

_____

5 I have a cheap phone. No mugger wants it.

_____

_____

6 The police were bored watching the criminal's house. They both fell asleep.

_____

_____

Consolidation

6 **Complete the article with the noun or adjective form of the verbs. Use *so* or *such* with the adjectives.**

Housewife frightens thieves

Mrs. Wallace had a big surprise on Friday morning when she went downstairs. Two [1]burglars (burgle) were walking out the front door with the family's new TV. Mrs. Wallace said, "When I saw them, I shouted for my husband. The [2]_____ (rob) were [3]_____ (surprise) that they dropped the TV. It was such an expensive TV—nearly $1,500!—that I got very angry with them. I was [4]_____ (anger) that I didn't have time to feel nervous! It was [5]_____ (annoy) that two [6]_____ (thieve) were in our house and they had broken our television."

By the time Mr. Wallace came downstairs, the burglars were [7]_____ (frighten) that they were trying to run away. Mr. Wallace said, "It was almost funny. My wife was [8]_____ (terrify) sight that I was scared, too! I called the police while my wife told off the thieves. The police arrived and arrested the two men."

11B I don't mind paying for music.

Vocabulary: Computer language

1 ★ Match the verbs (1–6) with the nouns (a–f).

1 attach
2 burn
3 crash
4 open
5 receive
6 surf

a) an e-mail
b) the Internet
c) an attachment
d) a CD
e) a file
f) a computer

2 ★ Use words from the box to label the diagram. There is one extra word.

• keyboard • laptop • memory stick • mouse • ~~PC~~ • printer • scanner • screen • website

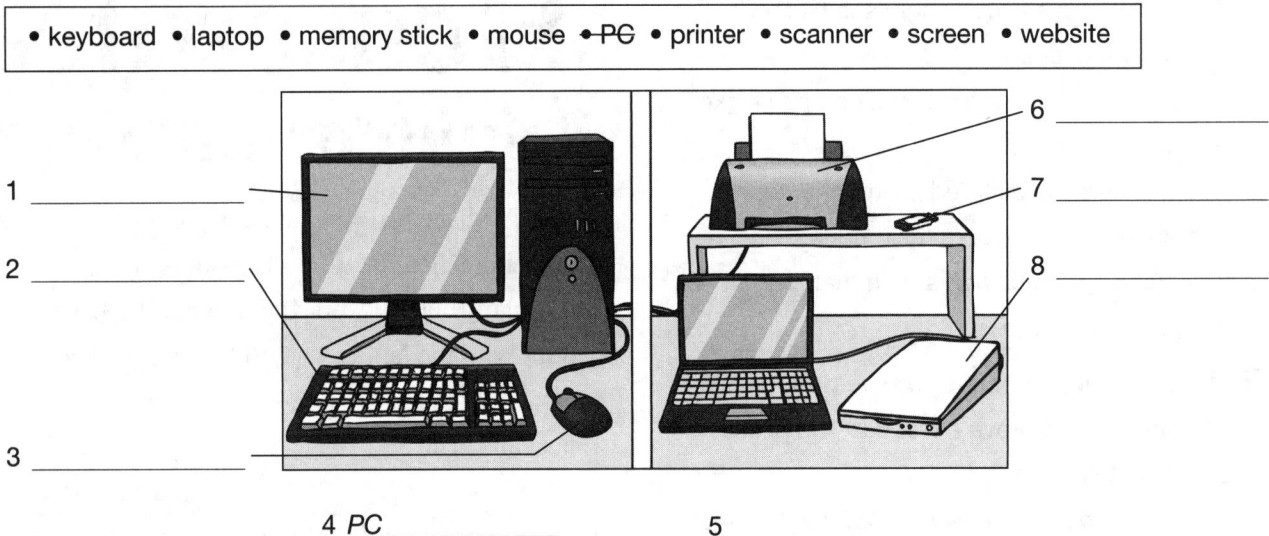

1 _____

2 _____

3 _____

4 _PC_____

5 _____

6 _____

7 _____

8 _____

3 ★★ Complete the conversation with computer words.

Customer: How do I **1** _connect_ to the Internet?

Salesperson: **2** W_____ is the easiest way to connect to the Internet.

Customer: What about viruses?

Salesperson: You need to install anti-virus **3** s_____ before you start to use the Internet.

Customer: Next question: My daughter wants to send me pictures of my grandchildren. How do I open them?

Salesperson: She'll **4** s_____ the photos as attachments by e-mail. Remember, never open an **5** a_____ if you don't know who sent it.

Customer: If I **6** r_____ an e-mail from someone I don't know, what do I do?

Salesperson: Don't open the e-mail, **7** d_____ it.

Customer: OK. Can I **8** d_____ music?

Salesperson: Yes, there are lots of **9** w_____ where you can buy music.

Customer: Thank you, you've been very helpful.

Grammar: Verb with infinitive or gerund

4 ★ **Circle the correct answers.**

1 Do you want *to play/playing* a video game?

2 My dad decided *to get/getting* another e-mail address.

3 I can't stand *to receive/receiving* e-mails from people I don't know.

4 We all agreed *to pay/paying* for the music we download.

5 The man in the store suggested *to get/getting* some anti-virus software.

6 Do you promise *to give/giving* me a gift?

5 ★ **Three more sentences have a mistake. Find them and correct them.**

1 ~~Does Jo admit to lose your memory stick?~~

Does Jo admit losing your memory stick?

2 Before the Internet, how did students manage to do homework?

_____

_____

3 Ellen enjoys talking to her friends online.

_____

_____

4 I miss using the Internet when I'm on vacation.

_____

_____

5 My brother always refuses sharing his computer.

_____

_____

6 I practice to speak French with my pen pal.

_____

_____

7 When you finish doing your homework, don't forget to save it.

_____

_____

8 You can't deny to download music from the Web!

_____

_____

6 ★★ **Complete the second sentence so it means the same as the first. Use the verb patterns in parentheses.**

1 I like watching TV while I eat my dinner. (verb + to + infinitive)

I like to watch TV while I eat my dinner.

2 They hate to get up early. (verb + gerund)

_____

3 She loves listening to music. (verb + to + infinitive)

_____

4 We started watching a movie. (verb + to + infinitive)

_____

5 Do you prefer doing research on the Internet? (verb + to + infinitive)

_____

Consolidation

7 **Complete the text with the correct form of the verbs in parentheses.**

Jon has decided **1** *to get* (get) a summer job. He hopes **2** _____ (save) enough money for a new laptop. He wants **3** _____ (work) in a computer store but he doesn't mind **4** _____ (take) a job in any store. Jon doesn't want **5** _____ (travel) very far. Although his mom has offered **6** _____ (give) him the bus fare he wants to avoid **7** _____ (pay) expensive bus fares.

At first, Jon expected **8** _____ (get) a job easily. However, it seems **9** _____ (be) difficult to get a job right now. He hasn't given up **10** _____ (look) yet. Every morning, he **11** _____ (look) on the Internet and in the newspaper. He hopes **12** _____ (find) a job soon.

Phrases

1 ★ Complete the conversations with the phrases in the box.

> • Hold on   • I just want to   • Don't worry   • I'm not wild about   • stuff

1 A: Come on, I'm bored. I hate shopping.

  B: _____ . I haven't looked at
    everything yet.

2 C: Do you like this shirt, Alan?

  D: No, _____ any of the _____ in
    this store, Mom.

3 E: I hope this doesn't take long.

  F: _____ . I'll be done in fifteen minutes.

4 G: Can you wait for me? _____ look at
    the jeans.

  H: Yes, I can.

Grammar: Auxiliary verbs with *so* and *neither*

2 ★ Match the sentences (1–10) with the replies (a–j).

1 We went to that new store in town.

2 I lost my scarf.

3 I'm not going shopping today.

4 I'm buying a new dress for the party.

5 I need some new gloves.

6 I don't want to wear my sweater.

7 I didn't like any of the clothes.

8 I can't find anything I want.

9 I can afford a new jacket this
  weekend.

10 I liked his new shirt.

a) Neither can I.

b) So did I.

c) I can't.

d) Neither am I.

e) I didn't.

f) I did.

g) Neither do I.

h) So did we.

i) I'm not.

j) So do I.

3 ★★ Write short replies. Use the correct auxiliary verbs.

1 I don't like that coat.   (disagree) _____ *I do.* _____

2 I love going shopping.   (disagree) _____

3 I can't make out the price. (agree) _____

4 I'm looking for a new
  winter coat.   (agree) _____

5 I've never worn a fur coat. (agree) _____

6 I have my gloves and
  scarf with me.   (disagree) _____

7 I bought the expensive
  sneakers.   (disagree) _____

8 I'm buying all my clothes
  in thrift shops now.   (agree) _____

Vocabulary: Clothes, accessories, styles, and patterns

4 ★ Label each picture with two words from the box.

> • baggy • cardigan • checkered • dotted
> • floral • gloves • plain • scarf • shirt
> • shorts • socks • striped • tight

1 *checkered socks*   2 _____

3 _____   4 _____

5 _____   6 _____

5 ★★ Complete the descriptions of the models' clothes.

James Kate

Greg

Ella

Greg is wearing 1 _baggy_ jeans with a plain

2 _____ . On his feet he is wearing 3 _____ .

Ella is in a plain 4 _____ with a 5 _____

T-shirt. On her feet she is wearing 6 _____ .

James is off to the beach in 7 _____ , a

8 _____ top and a pair of 9 _____ .

Kate is looking very fancy in a 10 _____ with a

11 _____ over it. She is wearing a small

12 _____ and dressy 13 _____ .

Use your English: Make and respond to requests

6 ★ Complete the conversations.

Conversation 1

A: 1 C_ould you_ open the door, please?

B: Yes, 2 s_____ .

Conversation 2

C: Can you tell me the way to the thrift shop, please?

D: Sorry, I'm 3 a_____ n_____ . I don't live here.

C: OK. 4 N_____ m_____ . I'm sure I'll find it.

Conversation 3

E: 5 W_____ you m_____ helping me?

F: Of course not, 6 n_____ p_____ .

Conversation 4

G: 7 D_____ you t_____ y_____ c_____ lend
me $10?

H: Sorry, 8 I'_____ a_____ I c_____ .

G: OK. It 9 d_____ m_____ . I'll ask Helena.

Consolidation

7 Some students are watching a school fashion show. Complete the conversation with the words and phrases in the box.

> • baggy pants • ~~Can I sit here~~ • Could I see them
> • dressy • Neither did I • so did I • tights
> • Yes, sure

Alex: 1 _Can I sit here_, please?

Kirsten: 2 _____ . I'll move my bag.

Alex: What do you think of the clothes?

Kirsten: I didn't like the 3 _____ with
sweaters.

Alex: 4 _____ but I liked some of the
hoodies.

Kirsten: Yes, 5 _____ .

Alex: Did you take any photographs?

Kirsten: Yes, I did.

Alex: 6 _____ , please?

Kirsten: Of course, no problem. They're on my phone.

Alex: All the 7 _____ clothes are in the
second half. I'm looking forward to that.

Kirsten: I'm not! I only wear casual clothes. I hate
wearing skirts and 8 _____ .

Extra challenge!

8 ★★★ Write a short response and add some information.

1 I think shoplifting is a serious crime.

So do I. Things are more expensive because

people steal from stores.

2 I don't worry about street crime.

_____

_____

3 We aren't allowed to wear jeans to school.

_____

_____

4 I can't afford to buy all the clothes I like.

_____

_____

Crime detection

Read

1a ★ Skim the article. What is the text mainly about?

a) developments in using DNA and police work

b) the use of science in police work

c) a criminal caught by DNA evidence

b ★ Now read the whole text and check your answer.

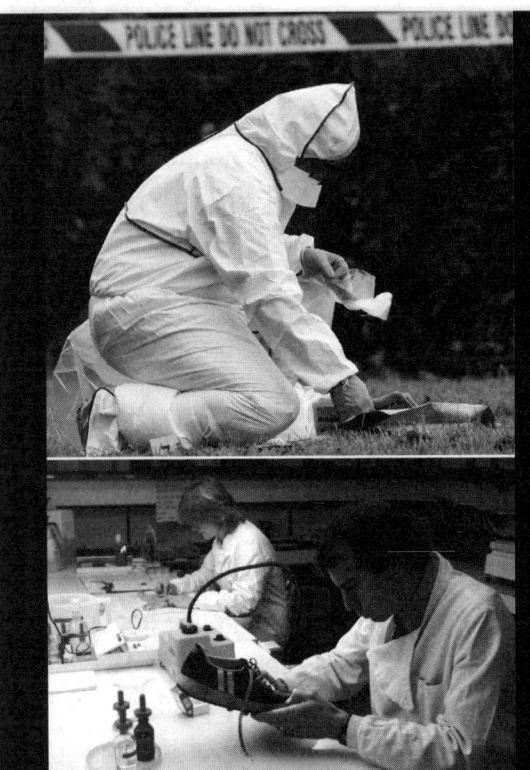

1 Modern science is helping police fight crime. In the 1950s, Watson and Crick discovered DNA. Years later, Jeffreys invented a way to match people with their DNA. Now, DNA fingerprinting has become so good that forensic scientists can find a match with only a small sample of DNA.

2 These advances mean that the police can investigate old, unsolved crimes. Forensic scientists can examine old evidence and find microscopic traces of DNA. Often they can find enough DNA to send criminals to prison. In some cases the criminals had escaped justice for more than twenty years.

3 DNA is like a fingerprint because, except for some twins, everyone's DNA is different. However, people in the same family have similar DNA. There have been successful prosecutions when DNA found at a crime scene has been similar to (but not the same as) a police DNA record. The police interviewed all the family members and arrested the correct person.

4 The police say, "Until we solve the crime, the case is never closed. DNA matching is getting better all the time so criminals have less chance of escaping justice. And the courts have freed people from prison when DNA evidence has proved they are innocent."

5 DNA is such a useful detection tool that some people want everyone's DNA "fingerprint" to be kept by the police. They say that it will make police work faster. However, other people think that this suggests that everyone is a criminal and it will damage our freedom.

New words

2 ★★ **Match the words and phrases (1–8) with the definitions (a–h).**

1 forensic (adj)
2 sample (n)
3 unsolved (adj)
4 examine (v)
5 microscopic (adj)
6 to escape justice (v)
7 prosecution (n)
8 tool (n)

a) to avoid being punished for a crime
b) too small to be seen
c) the action of taking someone to court
d) about scientific tests to help the police find criminals
e) to look at something carefully
f) a problem or crime where the answer hasn't been found
g) a piece of equipment or a skill
h) a very small part of something used for a scientific study

Comprehension

3 ★★ **Answer** *true* **(T),** *false* **(F), or** *don't know* **(DK).**

1 Police used DNA evidence in the 1950s. ☐
2 The amount of DNA needed for evidence is getting smaller. ☐
3 The people in a family have very different DNA. ☐
4 The Seattle police have three million DNA samples. ☐
5 DNA can only be used to solve twenty-first century crimes. ☐
6 Some people have proved their innocence with DNA evidence. ☐
7 All honest people want the police to keep a sample of everyone's DNA. ☐

Listen

4 ★ (13) **Listen and choose the correct answers.**

1 The woman was watching *TV / a webcam*.
2 She saw the boys *steal / break into* a car.
3 The police *arrested / didn't arrest* the thieves.

5 ★★ **Listen again and complete the notes.**

Names: Kyle McCormick, Aaron Highsmith
Crime: ¹b_____ into a car, took ²_____, _____, _____
Witness: in U.S.! saw the crime on her ³_____
Police received ⁴_____ from the witness, arrested the boys. Judge sent them to prison for ⁵_____.

Write

6 ★★ **A reporter made these notes in court. Use the notes to write a newspaper story on a piece of paper.**

Name: Antonia Lewis   Crime: shoplifting
Notes:
• May 4: suspect left Alphamax Clothes on Pike Street
• Store alarm went off
• Suspect caught by store detective
• Found a pair of jeans, a sweater, and a baseball hat in her bag
• Guilty, punishment 50 hours community service

On May 4, Antonia Lewis left...

They had to make a new rule.

Vocabulary: Sports

1a ★ Use the words in the box to label the pictures.

> • athlete • ~~ball~~ • basket • bat • coach • glove
> • goalkeeper • helmet • net • racket • referee
> • (shin) guards • spectator • umpire

1 *ball*

2 ___

3 ___

4 ___

5 ___   6 ___

7 ___

8 ___

9 ___   10 ___

11 ___

12 ___   13 ___

14 ___

b ★★ Look at the pictures on the left. Now write the names of three of the sports.

1 b _ _ _ _ _ _ _ _ _ _ _

2 t _ _ _ _ _ _   3 s _ _ _ _ _ _

2 ★ Choose the correct answers.

Now the sports news.

Soccer: Italy played Spain in Madrid last night. The **1** _a_ went into overtime when the two teams **2** ___ after ninety minutes. Italy finally **3** ___ the game when their number one player **4** ___ a goal. He **5** ___ the ball into the net after twenty-five minutes of overtime. The Winter Olympics and speed ice-skating: The American team **6** ___ their **7** ___ , the Austrian team, by 2.5 seconds. The American team has **8** ___ more medals than any other country in this year's Winter Olympics.

1 (a) game   b) team   c) umpire

2 a) won   b) tied   c) lost

3 a) played b) lost   c) won

4 a) hit   b) scored   c) threw

5 a) kicked b) passed   c) scored

6 a) won   b) beat   c) drew

7 a) team   b) spectators c) opponents

8 a) scored b) won   c) played

3 ★★ **Write the names of the sports. Include the correct verb:** *play, do,* **or** *go.*

1 *go windsurfing*

2 _____

3 _____

4 _____

5 _____

6 _____

Grammar: Rules and obligations: *must / have to*

4 ★ **Circle the correct answers.**

Race car drivers

- 1 *don't have to/can't* start before the signal.

- 2 *can't/must* cause an accident.

- 3 *don't have to/can't* be engineers.

At the 1948 Olympics, the athletes

- 4 *must/had to* sleep in camps and schools.

- 5 *had/have* to bring their own equipment and towels.

- 6 *couldn't/didn't have to* stay in an Olympic village.

5 ★★ **Complete the rules for a modern skateboard park and nineteenth-century tennis.**

Skateboarders

1 *must* wear helmets and guards.

2 _____ wear special clothes.

3 _____ do dangerous jumps.

Women tennis players

4 _____ wear long skirts.

5 _____ wear hats.

Men tennis players

6 _____ wear a jacket.

7 _____ wear long pants.

Consolidation

6 **Complete the text with the phrases and sentences in the box.**

- lose a point
- a player must score four points
- ~~an indoor court~~
- the first ball must hit the wall
- if the score is 5–5
- the rackets are made of

Real tennis

Real (or "royal") tennis is a very old game from the fifteenth century. It is played on 1 *an indoor court* with four walls. 2 _____ wood and the balls are handmade. When a game starts, 3 _____ before it hits the floor. If a player's ball hits his or her opponent, they 4 _____ . The scoring is the same as for modern tennis. To win a game 5 _____ and have two points more than his or her opponent. The first player to win six games is the winner. 6 _____ , the eleventh game decides who is the winner.

You'd better go to the hospital.

Phrases

1 ★ **Match the sentences (1–5) with the replies (a–e).**

1 He stood on my toy car and he twisted his ankle.

2 I cut my hand.

3 Are you going ice-skating tomorrow?

4 Look out! There's a car coming.

a) No, I can't make it.

b) It looks serious. You'd better put a bandage on it.

c) You shouldn't leave your toys on the floor!

d) Thank you—he was driving too fast!

Vocabulary: Injuries and treatment

2 ★ **Circle the words that don't belong.**

1 thumb finger (eye) toe

2 wrist hand tooth arm

3 ankle hair knee foot

4 face ear mouth nose

5 head neck muscle shoulder

6 stomach elbow back chest

3 ★★ **Label the pictures.**

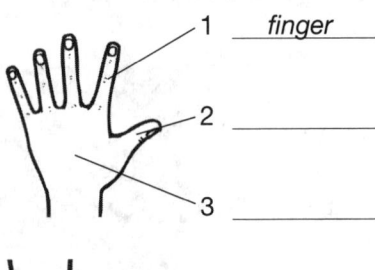

1 _finger_

2 _____

3 _____

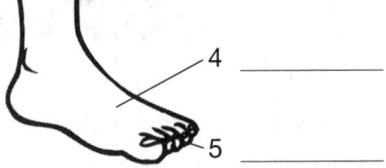

4 _____

5 _____

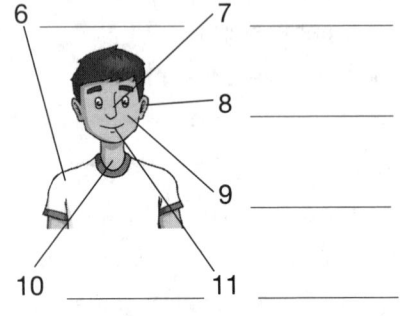

6 _____ 7 _____

8 _____

9 _____

10 _____ 11 _____

4 ★ **Rearrange the letters to make words.**

 1 mbaanceul

ambulance

 2 tohs

_____

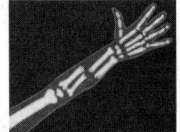 3 yrxa-

_____

 4 lerpnikial

_____

5 raemc

_____

6 ngeabad

_____

5 ★★ **What is wrong with the people in the doctor's waiting room?**

1 She b_roke_ her a_rm_ .

2 He has a s_____ .

3 He c_____ his h_____ .

4 She t_____ her a_____ .

5 He has a lot of i_____ b_____ .

6 She has an e_____ .

7 He has a n_____ .

Grammar: *should/ought to/ had better*

6 ★ Circle the correct answers.

1 You *shouldn't*/*had better* go to the hospital if you have a cold.

2 You *should/ought not to* sit down if you are feeling faint.

3 People *ought to/shouldn't* take too many painkillers.

4 You *shouldn't/ought to* go to bed if you don't feel very well.

5 If you break a tooth, you *ought to/had better not* make a dentist appointment.

6 That's a nasty sting. *You shouldn't/You'd better* put some cream on it.

7 ★★ Read the problems and write advice. Use the cues.

1 My knee hurts. (should(n't) + rest/go skiing)
You should rest. You shouldn't go skiing.

2 I have a temperature. (should(n't) + go ice-skating/drink lots of water)
_____
_____

3 I twisted my ankle. (better (not) + play basketball/put a bandage on it)
_____
_____

4 I think I pulled a muscle in my back. (ought+ take a break from gymnastics)
_____
_____

5 I have an awful headache. (should(n't) + stop listening to loud music/ spend all your time indoors)
_____
_____

6 I burned my hand. (should(n't) + put your hand in cold water / be so careless)
_____
_____

Use your English: Ask for and give advice

8 ★ Match the beginnings (1–6) with the endings (a–f).

1 What do you think   a) about that.

2 Do you think   b) getting shots

3 I think you ought   c) I should go to the dentist?

4 If I were you,   d) to go to the hospital.

5 I don't like   e) I should do?

6 I'm not sure   f) I'd call an ambulance.

9 ★★ Complete the conversations.

Conversation 1

A: I have an awful cough. What **1** s*hould* I do?

B: If I **2** w_____ y_____, I'd go to the pharmacy for some cough medicine.

A: **3** G_____ i_____a, thank you.

Conversation 2

C: I fell skateboarding and I broke a tooth. What **4** d_____ you t_____ I s_____ d_____ ?

D: You **5** h_____ b_____ go to the dentist.

Consolidation

10 Choose the correct answers.

Alex: Mom, I don't feel well. I think **1** _c_ go to school today.

Mom: What's the problem?

Alex: I have a **2** ____ throat.

Mom: Your throat *is* red. Do you have a **3** ____ ?

Alex: I think so. I have a **4** ____ .

Mom: I think you have a cold. **5** ____ spend the day in bed.

Alex: I'm **6** ____ about that. I think I should rest on the sofa.

Mom: If **7** ____ , I'd go to bed.

Alex: Oh Mom, that's boring.

Mom: If you're sick, go to bed. If you're not sick, go to school.

Alex: Yes, I suppose you're right. I'll go to bed.

1 a) I ought to   b) I'd better   c) I shouldn't

2 a) sprained   b) sore   c) twisted

3 a) temperature   b) bandage   c) pulled muscle

4 a) headache   b) insect bite   c) cut

5 a) You shouldn't   b) You oughtn't   c) You'd better

6 a) right   b) silly   c) not sure

7 a) I should   b) I were you   c) I'm right

Grammar and vocabulary:
Adjectives with prepositions

1 ★ **Choose the correct answers.**

1 I'd never flown before so I was a bit worried _b_ the flight.
   a) at   (b) about)   c) of

2 The children were fascinated ___ the animals in the zoo.
   a) from   b) by   c) with

3 A monkey is similar ___ an ape.
   a) to   b) with   c) from

4 She doesn't want to go to Beijing because she isn't crazy ___ Chinese food.
   a) with   b) about   c) on

5 After a day on Fifth Avenue we were all tired ___ shopping.
   a) at   b) of   c) about

6 Jenna was annoyed ___ leaving the party early.
   a) about   b) from   c) with

7 Her e-mail address is different ___ her old one.
   a) at   b) from   c) with

8 I'm not very good ___ math so I find time differences confusing!
   a) on   b) to   c) at

9 Is Polly interested ___ visiting Jenna in London?
   a) with   b) for   c) in

2 ★★ **Complete the second sentence so it means the same as the first.**

1 People visit New York to see the Statue of Liberty.
   New York is famous _for the Statue of Liberty_ .

2 My aunt and uncle are very happy because of their new baby.
   My aunt and uncle are proud _____
   _____ .

3 My little brother doesn't like the dark.
   My little brother is afraid _____ .

4 She can't sing!
   She is bad _____ .

5 Do you like jazz music a lot?
   Are you crazy _____ ?

6 It's your fault you got bad grades.
   You are responsible _____ .

7 You shouldn't get stressed when you go to the dentist.
   You shouldn't worry _____ .

8 I feel unhappy because I broke your phone.
   I'm sorry _____ .

9 We were amazed when we saw our test results.
   We were surprised _____ .

3 ★★ **Write sentences.**

1 I / be / responsible / guarding Buckingham Palace in London
   I am responsible for guarding Buckingham Palace in London.

2 we / be / famous / our red jackets and large fur hats
   _____
   _____

3 I / be / proud / working at Buckingham Palace

_____

_____

4 tourists / be / fascinated / my uniform

_____

_____

5 I / get / fed up / tourists taking my picture

_____

_____

6 I / not be / afraid / anyone or anything

_____

_____

Consolidation

4 Complete the e-mail with the adjective form of the words in parentheses and the correct prepositions.

From:	Ed
To:	Carl

Hi Carl!

I was just on an adventure vacation in Vancouver. The vacation was very ¹*different from* (differ) anything I'd done before. I was ² _____ (surprise) how much I enjoyed it.

We camped in some mountains which are ³ _____ (famous) wildlife. I was ⁴ _____ (fascinate) the animals. We saw a wild cat one day! I'm very ⁵ _____ (pride) myself because I tried climbing. As you know, I'm ⁶ _____ (frighten) heights so I was very brave. Now, I'm ⁷ _____ (interest) learning to climb so I'm going to our local climbing wall every week.

Write soon.

Love,

Ed

Extra challenge!

5 ★★★ Complete the conversations. Use the treatments in the box and your own ideas.

> • put some ice on it • take some painkillers
> • go to bed • see a dentist

Conversation 1

School nurse: What's the matter with you?

Student 1:   I hurt my elbow playing tennis.

School nurse: You should 1 *put some ice on it and take some painkillers* .

Conversation 2

Student 2:   I have a bad toothache.

School nurse: You'd better 2 _____

_____ .

Student 2:   I don't like going to the dentist.

School nurse: You shouldn't be 3 _____

of the dentist.

Conversation 3

Student 3:   I fell down and I cut my knee.

School nurse: I'll 4 _____ .

You'll have to rest your leg for two days.

Student 3:   I'm really 5 _____

about this. I wanted to play soccer today.

School nurse: No, you can't play today. I can't be responsible for you getting an infection.

Conversation 4

Student 4:   I have a temperature and a headache.

School nurse: You ought to 6 _____

_____ .

Student 4:   But I need to study for my tests next week.

School nurse: You shouldn't 7 _____

about your school work if you've got the flu.

12D Values for living

INTEGRATED
CONSOLIDATION
SKILLS

The adventure

Read

1 ★ Read the e-mail and choose the correct answers.

The e-mail is:

1 *from/to* the expedition organizer.

2 *to give/ask for* information.

3 friendly *and informal/but formal*.

From:	Tania Morales
To:	Ann Davidson

From: tania.morales@gap4adventure.com
To: Ann Davidson
Sent: Tuesday, May 31   10:43 AM
Subject: Teach and Explore Adventure

Dear Ann,

East Africa: Two-month teach and explore adventure
Welcome to your Gap Adventure! Thank you for your deposit of $200. You are booked on our Teach and Explore Adventure in East Africa which leaves on September 1. You must pay the balance of the money ($1,800) two months before you leave (July 1).
In preparation for your adventure, you will need to get:

• a passport
• visas
• vaccinations against tropical illnesses (visit the Centers for Disease Control and
   Prevention website for up-to-date information).

On our website www.gap4adventure.com, you will find a detailed list of essential clothes and equipment, for example, boots and a backpack. There is also a list of other things you may want to take, for example, a camera and a notebook.
It's useful to practice packing and carrying your backpack before you leave. Remember, you will have to carry everything you take! Although we don't suggest any special fitness training, you ought to wear your boots for a few weeks before the trip. There is nothing worse than blisters when you have to walk ten miles.

Sincerely,

Tania Morales

Tania Morales
Group Leader
tania.morales@gap4adventure.com

New words

2 ★★ Find the new words (1–7) in the text and decide if they are adjectives or nouns. Then match the words with the definitions (a–g).

1 deposit _____noun_____   a) from the hottest parts of the world

2 balance _____   b) part of the price you pay first so the thing isn't sold to another person

3 visa _____   c) a shot that protects you from illness

4 vaccination _____   d) liquid under your skin caused by rubbing

5 tropical _____   e) the rest of the money

6 essential _____   f) an official mark in your passport which allows you to travel in a country

7 blister(s) _____   g) very important and necessary

Comprehension

3 ★★ Answer _true_ (T) or _false_ (F).

1 Ann has paid for all of her expedition. ☐

2 Before Ann goes to East Africa, she
   must get some shots. ☐

3 The letter tells Ann how many
   vaccinations to get. ☐

4 Gap Adventure says travelers get
   to take boots. ☐

5 It's not important to practice packing
   and carrying your backpack. ☐

6 Travelers must take a camera with
   them. ☐

7 To enjoy the trip you don't have to do
   any special training. ☐

Listen

> **Listening tip: Prepare to listen**
>
> Before you listen, look at the task. This will
> help focus your listening.

4 ★ (14) Listen and choose the correct answers.

1 Ann is talking to her _mom/dad_.

2 They are talking about _the e-mail/her job_.

3 _They have both read/only Ann has read_ the
   e-mail.

5 ★★ Listen again. Choose the correct answers.

1 Ann has a job in a ___ .
   a) restaurant   b) movie theater   c) shop

2 When a customer gives a waiter extra money, it's ___ .
   a) five dollars   b) a promise   c) a tip

3 Ann's dad ___ what a visa is.
   a) doesn't know   b) explains   c) wants to know

4 Ann is ___ of shots.
   a) afraid   b) bad   c) fed up

5 Ann's dad says ___ have the shots.
   a) she'd better   b) she must   c) she should

6 She ___ at the website.
   a) has looked   b) is going to look   c) might look

7 She's going to ___ Gap Adventure later.
   a) e-mail   b) call   c) text

8 She ___ speaking to someone who has been to
   Africa.
   a) was fascinated by   b) is interested in
   c) is worried about

Write

6 ★★ On a piece of paper, write Ann's e-mail to Gap Adventure.

- Write the name of the expedition in the subject line.
- Say thank you for the e-mail.
- Explain that you have two questions.
- Ask from which airport the flight will leave.
- Ask for the name and phone number of someone who has done the trip before.
- End in a friendly, polite way.

Grammar Bank

Welcome to the **Grammar Bank!**

- The **Grammar Bank** gives you extra practice on all the grammar points in each unit of the Student Book.

- At the start of each unit in the Grammar Bank, there is a *Grammar summary* page with examples of all the grammar points from the unit and notes about grammar rules. You can use these to help you when you are doing an exercise and as a check when you are reviewing.

- A set of *Grammar practice* exercises follows each Grammar summary. You can use these exercises as a follow-up to the exercises in the Workbook, or you can use them later to help you review.

- At the end of each unit is a Consolidation exercise, which practices all the grammar points from the unit.

Grammar Summary

Simple present

Affirmative
I/You/We/They **know** lots of people.
He/She/It **lives** in Seattle.

Negative
I/You/We/They **don't know** many people.
He/She/It **doesn't live** in Seattle.

Questions
Does he **like** the youth club?
Do we **go** to the same school?

Short answers
Yes, he **does**. No, he **doesn't**.
Yes, we **do**. No, we **don't**.

Wh- questions
Where **do** you **hang out**? Why **is** he selfish?

Present continuous

Affirmative
I**'m waiting** for a friend.
He/She/It**'s running** in the park.
You/We/They**'re listening** to music.

Negative
I**'m not waiting** for a friend.
He/She/It **isn't running** in the park.
You/We/They **aren't listening** to music.

Questions
Am I **sitting** here?
Is she **doing** her homework?
Are they **waiting** for a bus?

Short answers
Yes, you **are**. No, you**'re not**.
Yes, she **is**. No, she **isn't**.
Yes, they **are**. No, they **aren't**.

Wh- questions
What **am** I **waiting** for? Why **are** you **asking**?
Where **is** he **living**?

Wh- questions

How do you say "bonjour" in English?
What is she doing?
When does the movie start?
Where is your dad working this month?
Which bands do you like?
Who are you hanging out with today?
Whose dictionary is this?
Why are you waiting here?

Notes
Simple present
Usage
- We use the simple present for permanent situations and routines.
- We often use adverbs like *never*, *sometimes*, *usually* with the simple present to show frequency.

Form
- For the third person singular affirmative we add *-s* to most verbs.
- *have* becomes *has*.
- We add *-es* to the auxiliary *do* in simple present negative sentences and questions. The main verb doesn't change.

Present continuous
Usage
- We use the present continuous for activities which are happening now or which are temporary.
- With the present continuous we use time expressions like *now, these days*.

Form
- We use the correct present tense form of *to be* + the gerund (*-ing* form) of the verb.

Non-action verbs
Usage
- With verbs that refer to states (not actions or processes), we usually use the simple form.
  - Senses: *see, feel, hear, smell, taste* (these are often used with *can*)
  - Thoughts/ideas: *believe, forget, know, mean, need, prefer, remember, think, understand, want*
  - Emotions: *hate, love, like*

Wh- question words
Form
- To form *wh-* questions we use question word/phrase + auxiliary verb + subject + infinitive without *to*.
- We use *do* when the question is about the object. *Who do you sit with in class?*
- With *to be* and other auxiliary verbs, we do not use *do*. *Why are you here?*

Simple past of regular verbs

Affirmative

I/You/He/She/It/We/They **studied** English last year.

Negative

I/You/He/She/It/We/They **didn't study** English last year.

Questions

Did it **help** you?

Short answers

Yes, it **did**.　　　　No, it **didn't**.

Wh- questions

When **did** I **call** you?

Simple past of irregular verbs

Affirmative

I/You/He/She/It/We/They **went** to the U.S. last month.

Negative

I/You/He/She/It/We/They **didn't go** to the U.S. last month.

Questions

Did he **go** to Idaho last summer?

Short answers

Yes, he **did**.　No, he **didn't**.

Wh- questions

When **did** she **meet** you?

Past continuous

Affirmative

I/He/She/It **was reading** a newspaper.
You/We/They **were walking** to school.

Negative

I/He/She/It **wasn't reading** a newspaper.
You/We/They **weren't walking** to school.

Questions

Was she **eating** lunch?
Were we **talking** on the phone?

Short answers

Yes, she **was**.　No, she **wasn't**.
Yes, we **were**.　No, we **weren't**.

Wh- questions

What **was** it **doing**?
Where **were** you **going**?

Notes

Simple past

Usage

- We use the simple past for single actions, repeated actions, and states completed in the past.

Form

- The verb is the same for all persons in the simple past.
- To form the simple past we add -ed to most regular verbs.
- To form negatives we use *didn't* + the infinitive without *to*.
- To form questions we use *did* + subject + the infinitive without *to*.

Past continuous

Usage

- We use the past continuous for past actions which:
  - lasted for a period of time.
    They were traveling for three months.
  - started before a simple past action.
    We were listening to music when the phone rang.
  - started before and continued after a time in the past.
    It was raining at six o'clock.

Form

- We form the past continuous with the correct past tense form of the verb *to be* + the gerund (-*ing* form) of the verb.

Past continuous and simple past

Usage

- We can use the past continuous and simple past together to talk about longer and shorter actions in the past. We use the past continuous for the longer action and the simple past for the shorter action.
- We use *while/as* (= a period of time) with the past continuous and *when* (= at that time) with the simple past.
  While he was waiting, he got the message.
  He was waiting **when** he got the message.
- With the simple past and the past continuous we use phrases like *yesterday (morning), last week/month*.

Grammar practice

Simple present

1 ★★ **Complete the sentences with the simple present form of the verbs in parentheses.**

1 He *doesn't like* (not like) swimming.

2 I _____ (not sit) with my best friend in class.

3 _____ the dog _____ (want) some water?

4 We usually _____ (do) our homework together.

5 _____ they _____ (take) the bus often?

6 He _____ (have) sandwiches for lunch every day.

2 ★★ **Use the adverbs of frequency in the box to complete the text about Alex.**

- always • never (×2) • often (×2)
- sometimes • ~~usually~~

	Mon	Tues	Wed	Thurs	Fri	Sat	Sun
Gets up at 7 o'clock	✓	✓	✓	✓	✓	✗	✗
Goes swimming	✗	✗	✗	✗	✗	✗	✗
Plays tennis	✓	✗	✓	✓	✗	✓	✓
Sees friends	✗	✓	✗	✗	✓	✓	✗
Watches TV	✓	✗	✓	✓	✗	✗	✓
Walks to school	✓	✓	✓	✓	✓	—	—

Alex **1** *usually* gets up at seven o'clock but on the weekends he **2** _____ gets up early. He **3** _____ walks to school. In the evenings he **4** _____ watches TV. During the week, he **5** _____ hangs out with his friends. He **6** _____ goes swimming but he **7** _____ plays tennis.

Present continuous

3 ★★ **Complete the conversation with the present continuous form of the verbs in parentheses.**

Rosa: Hi! What **1** *are you doing* (do)?

Simon: I **2** _____ (wait) for the bus.

Rosa: You sound unhappy. Why?

Simon: It **3** _____ (rain) and I **4** _____ (get) very wet! What **5** _____ you _____ (do)?

Rosa: Jo and I **6** _____ (hang out) at her house. We **7** _____ (not do) anything special.

Simon: My bus is here! Bye!

4 ★★ **Complete the sentences with the present continuous form of the verbs in the box.**

- do • learn • not play • not speak • sleep
- ~~walk~~ • work

1 We *'re walking* to school.

2 The cat _____ in the yard.

3 I _____ in a store this summer.

4 She _____ tennis today because she's sick.

5 I don't know what that language is but they _____ French!

6 _____ you _____ a lot of new vocabulary in your English class?

7 Look at that man! What _____ he _____ ?

Simple present and present continuous

5 ★★ **Write questions and short answers in your notebook. Use the simple present or the present continuous.**

1 your cat / like / milk ? Yes

2 Ben and Alice / watch / a movie right now ? Yes

3 you / speak / four languages ? No

4 you and Oliver / talk / about the concert ? Yes

Wh- and *How* questions

6 ★ **Complete the conversations with question words.**

1 W *h e r e* do your grandparents live?

In an apartment near the station.

2 W _ _ is your best friend?

It's Sam Kennedy.

3 H _ _ do you say "cookie" in British English?

You say "biscuit."

4 W _ _ _ is your favorite food?

Chicken and rice!

5 H _ _ long is the movie?

About two hours.

6 H _ _ m _ _ _ students are in your class?

There are thirty.

7 W _ _ are you walking to school today?

Because my bicycle is broken.

7 ★★ **Complete the conversation with questions.**

Jane: (school / go ?) 1 *Which school do you go to?*

Sally: I go to Northwest High School.

Jane: (sit with in class ?)

2 _____

Sally: My best friend, Helena.

Jane: (she / like ?)

3 _____

Sally: She's cheerful and she's very smart.

Jane: (see her ?)

4 _____

Sally: Everyday! I see her at school and we go to the youth club on the weekends.

Jane: (be the youth club ?)

5 _____

Sally: It's only a mile from my house.

Jane: (do there ?)

6 _____

Sally: We see our friends, watch DVDs, or play basketball.

Simple past

8 ★★ **Complete the e-mail with the simple past form of the verbs in the box.**

> • be (×3) • ~~do~~ • have (×2) • make • not finish
> • not win • play • see • watch

From:	Ben
To:	Uncle Jake
☰▾ Date:	Monday, September 16

Hi Uncle Jake!

What ¹*did* you *do* last weekend? ² _____ you _____ a good time?

My weekend ³ _____ cool! It ⁴ _____ my birthday on Saturday. I ⁵ _____ soccer with my friends. My team ⁶ _____ but we ⁷ _____ fun. Then we ⁸ _____ pizzas for my birthday party. We ⁹ _____ *Avatar* on television. ¹⁰ _____ you _____ it?

I ¹¹ _____ my homework over the weekend so my teachers ¹² _____ angry today.

Love,

Ben

Past continuous

9 ★★ **Write sentences. Use the past continuous.**

What was your family doing at 8:00 this morning?

1 my brother / walk / to school.

My brother was walking to school.

2 I / watch / television

_____

3 I / not watch / the news. / I / watch / cartoons.

_____

4 my mother / read / e-mail.

_____

5 my father / eat / breakfast.

_____

6 my sisters / not eat / breakfast. / they / do / their homework.

_____

10 ★★ Complete the text with the past continuous form of the verbs in the box.

> • do • not play • play • read • sleep
> • talk • watch

Last night at 8:00, my mom **1** _was reading_ the newspaper. My dad **2** _____ to a friend. My sister and I **3** _____ video games. My brother **4** _____ with us, he **5** _____ TV. What **6** _____ my grandfather _____ ? He **7** _____ !

Simple past and past continuous

11 ★★ Complete the sentences with the simple past or the past continuous form of the verbs.

1 When I _woke up_ (wake up), my dad was making breakfast.

2 As I was taking a shower, I _____ (hear) the phone ring.

3 My mom _____ (talk) on the phone when I came downstairs.

4 When I _____ (go) into the kitchen, Dad was reading the newspaper.

5 While I was waiting for my friend, I _____ (check) my homework.

6 I _____ (walk) to my first class when I _____ (see) my best friend.

12 ★★ Complete the text with the correct form of the verbs in the box.

> • buy • decide • go • have • need • return
> • see • take • tell • walk

Last Saturday I **1** _went_ into town because I **2** _____ a birthday present for my little sister. As I **3** _____ along Mill Street, I **4** _____ a friend from school in a café. He **5** _____ a drink and a sandwich. I **6** _____ to have some lunch with him. While I **7** _____ him why I was in town, he **8** _____ a Wallace and Gromit DVD from his bag. His aunt **9** _____ it for his birthday but he **10** _____ it to the store. He said "Please give it to your sister." It was very generous!

Consolidation

13 Complete the text with the correct form of the verbs in parentheses. Use the simple present, present continuous, simple past, or past continuous.

My name **1** _is_ (be) Maria and I **2** _____ (live) in Portland. My mom and dad **3** _____ (work) in New York for two weeks so I **4** _____ (stay) with my aunt and uncle. They're cool! Yesterday, they **5** _____ (take) me and a friend for pizza. While we **6** _____ (walk) to the restaurant we **7** _____ (see) Bono in the street! My uncle **8** _____ (want) to speak to him but my aunt **9** _____ (not think) it was a good idea.

My big brother, Joe, is married so he **10** _____ (not live) with us. He and his wife **11** _____ (study) languages at a university. This semester they **12** _____ (not be) at school because they **13** _____ (live) in Italy for three months. Mom and I **14** _____ (go) there six weeks ago. Dad **15** _____ (not go) with us because he **16** _____ (finish) some work.

Grammar summary

Future with *be going to*

Affirmative

I**'m going to buy** a guitar.
He/She/It **is going to be** a musician.
You/We/They**'re going to listen** to some jazz.

Negative

I**'m not going to buy** a guitar.
He/She/It **isn't going to be** a musician.
You/We/They **aren't going to** listen to any jazz.

Questions

Is he **going to buy** a CD?
Are we **going to download** some music?

Short answers

Yes, he **is**.   No, he **isn't**.
Yes, we **are**.   No, we **aren't**.

Future with *will*

Affirmative

I/You/He/She/It/We/They**'ll (will) meet** you at the concert.

Negative

I/You/He/She/It/We/They **won't (will not) see** you tomorrow.

Questions

Will they **buy** a guitar?

Short answers

Yes, they **will**. No, they **won't (will not)**.

Present continuous form for fixed future arrangements

Affirmative

I**'m flying** to Canada on Saturday.

Negative

He/She/It **isn't having** dinner with us tomorrow.

Questions

Are you **studying** French next year?

Short answers

Yes, **I am**.   No, **I'm not**.

Notes

Future with *be going to*

Usage

- We use *going to* for plans, intentions, and predictions in the future based on present evidence.

Form

- We use the correct form of the verb *to be* + *going to* + infinitive without *to*.
- When we use *going to* with *to go*, we often leave out the verb *to go*. Both forms are correct, but it sounds more natural without *to go*.

Future with *will*

Usage

- We use *will* for predictions and decisions about the future based on ideas and thoughts.

Form

- We use *will/won't* + infinitive without *to*.
- We don't need another auxiliary verb in *will* questions and negatives.

Present continuous form for fixed future arrangements

Usage

- We use the present continuous for fixed plans in the future.
- With the present continuous for future arrangements, we often use time adverbials like *next week, on the weekend, tomorrow, in December* to show that the activity is in the future.

Form

See Unit 1.

Comparison of adjectives

Regular short adjectives

Adjective	Comparative	Superlative
sad	sadder than	the saddest
nice	much nicer than	the nicest
friendly	(not) as friendly as	the friendliest

Regular long adjectives

Adjective	Comparative	Superlative
amazing	more/less amazing than	the most/least amazing
interesting	much more/less interesting than	the most/least interesting
exciting	(not) as exciting as	the most/least exciting

Irregular adjectives

Adjective	Comparative	Superlative
good	(much) better than (not) as good as	the best
bad	(much) worse than (not) as bad as	the worst

Comparison of adjectives

Usage

- We use comparative + *than* to compare two things.
- To make a comparison between two things stronger, we use *much* before the comparative adjective.
- We use *as* + adjective + *as* to say two things are the same.
- We use (*not*) *as* + adjective + *as* to say two things are different.
- We use *the* + superlative to compare
  - a person or thing with two or more other people or things.
  - one thing with its whole group.

Spelling rules

- After one syllable adjectives:
  - usually, add -*er* or -*est*
  - after -*e*, add -*r* or -*st*
  - after one vowel and one consonant, double the consonant and add -*er* or -*est*
- After two syllable adjectives:
  - after a vowel sound, add -*er* or -*est*
  - ending in -*y*, change to *i* and add -*er* or -*est*
- For all other two syllable or longer adjectives, use *more/most* + adjective

Grammar practice

Future with *be going to* and *will*

1 ★★ Complete the e-mail with the correct form of *going to* or *will* and the verbs in the box.

> • be (×2) • buy • ~~drive~~ • leave • meet
> • not need • not take • send • write

| From: | Stefan |
| To: | Katy |

Hi Katy,

I'm writing this in an Internet café in Olympia. I'm staying with Louis and tomorrow we ¹*'re going to drive* to Tacoma for the rock festival! I read that there ² _____ about 140,000 people there!

Later today, we ³ _____ a tent. Louis wants to buy a big one but I think we ⁴ _____ it. We ⁵ _____ watching the bands most of the time. There are lots of people selling food at the festival so we ⁶ _____ any food with us.

I think we ⁷ _____ early in the morning so we have plenty of time to find the campsite. Louis ⁸ _____ his brother Jason there. I think Jason ⁹ _____ a text message with his tent's "address"!

I ¹⁰ _____ again next week and tell you all about the festival.

Love,

Stefan

Present continuous form for fixed future arrangements

2 ★★ Complete the sentences with the present continuous form of the verbs in parentheses.

head band

Summer Schedule

Tour dates
April 21, 22 Seattle
April 23, 24 Portland
April 27, 28 Eureka
April 29, 30 San Francisco

May 4–10 London Recording Studios, U.K.

May 15 Charity concert, Dublin

June Head Band's summer vacation!

1 The band *'s visiting* (visit) the U.S. in April.
2 They _____ (not play) in Los Angeles.
3 _____ the band _____ (go) to Chicago?
4 The band _____ (play) in Seattle first.
5 In May, they _____ (record) a new album.
6 On May 15, they _____ (fly) to Dublin.
7 The band _____ (not work) in June.

3 ★★ Complete the text with the present continuous form of the verbs in the box.

> • ride • ~~do~~ • go • not go • start • take (×2) • work

I have lots of plans this year. Next week, I ₁ *'m doing* some chores. After that, my friends and I ₂ _____ our bikes fifty miles to raise money for charity. My parents ₃ _____ us skiing in December so we ₄ _____ on vacation this summer. In August, I ₅ _____ in a store so I can earn some money. In November, I ₆ _____ some skiing lessons at an indoor ski school. Next semester my friends and I ₇ _____ a new school. I'm very excited about it. It's much bigger than our old school so we're going to meet lots of new people. ₈ _____ you _____ to a new school, too?

Comparison of adjectives

4 ★★ Write sentences comparing the two theaters. Use the comparative form of the adjectives with *much* or *not as . . . as.*

1 Cinema Heaven / busy / The Grand

Cinema Heaven is much busier than The Grand.

2 Cinema Heaven / small / The Grand

_____

3 The food at The Grand / good / the food at Cinema Heaven

_____

4 The Grand / old / Cinema Heaven

_____

5 Cinema Heaven / nice / The Grand

_____

5 ★★ Complete the text with superlative adjectives.

The Ritz Theater is 1 *the oldest* (old) movie theater in our town and it is also 2 _____ (small). There are only forty seats and they are 3 _____ (bad) seats in the world. They are the original seats from 1932 and they are so uncomfortable!

However, the theater is very popular because it shows 4 _____ (good) old movies from the 1930s and 40s. Last year, The Ritz had a comedy festival and they showed 5 _____ (funny) movies ever made.

6 ★★ Complete the text with comparatives and superlatives.

Name	Voice	Songs	Clothes
Crash Lee	XX	XXXX	✓✓✓✓✓✓
Di-Anna	XXXX	XX	✓✓✓✓
RV	XXXXXXXX	XXXXXXXX	✓✓✓✓✓

All three musicians are terrible! Crash Lee's voice is bad but Di-Anna's is 1 *much worse than* his. RV is 2 _____ musician of them all.

Their songs are boring. Di-Anna's songs are 3 _____ Crash Lee's or RV's. RV's songs are 4 _____ .

They all wear fantastic clothes. Crash Lee wears 5 _____ clothes. RV's clothes are 6 _____ Di-Anna's.

Consolidation

7 Complete the article with the correct form of the adjectives and verbs in parentheses.

Young Musician Competition

The winners of this year's Young Musician Competition are Jane Marshall, Eric Yeung, and Carlos Moreno.

Jane Marshall is twelve years old and she is 1 *the youngest* (young) winner in the history of the competition. She said, "It was 2 _____ (scary) I expected. It was easy! It was 3 _____ (fantastic) experience. I 4 _____ (be) here again next year!"

Eric Yeung said, "When I won, it was 5 _____ (awesome) moment of my life! Next month, I 6 _____ (play) in another competition. I was scared, but I feel very 7 _____ (confident) now."

Carlos Moreno, wasn't 8 _____ (happy) everyone else. "It was 9 _____ (bad) day of my life. I was so scared! I 10 _____ (play) next year, that's for sure!"

Grammar summary

Present perfect

Affirmative
I/You/We/They**'ve lived** here for two months.
He/She/It**'s been** in the yard since lunchtime.

Negative
I/You/We/They **haven't lived** here for two months.
He/She/It **hasn't been** in the yard since lunchtime.

Questions
Have **you cooked** dinner?
Has **it eaten** the fish?

Short answers
Yes, I **have**.   No, I **haven't**.
Yes, it **has**.   No, it **hasn't**.

Wh- questions
What **have** we **done**?
Where **has** he **put** the book?

Present perfect with *ever* and *never*
Have you **ever** been to Chile?
She's **never** eaten Japanese food.

Present perfect with *already* and *yet*
We've **already** done our homework.
Has it stopped raining **yet**?

Notes
Present perfect
Usage
• We use the present perfect to connect past events with the present.
  - A past experience when we don't say when it happened:
    I've been to Spain. = I went to Spain in the **past**, **now** I have the experience.
  - Things which started in the past and are still true:
    We've been friends for six years. = We became friends in the **past**, we are still friends **now**.

Form
• We use the correct present tense form of *have* + past participle.

Present perfect with *ever, never, already,* and *yet*
Usage
• We use the present perfect with
  - *ever* in questions to mean *at any time in your life*.
  - *never* in positive sentences to mean *at no time in my life*.
  - *already* in positive sentences to emphasize that something has happened before now.
  - *yet* at the end of negative sentences and questions to mean *up to now*.

Restrictive adjective clauses with *who, that, whose, where*

People (who/that)
I have a friend **who** e-mails me every day.
(subject)
Work with the person **(who/that)** you sit next to in class.
(object)

Things (that)
My friend gave me some advice **that** helped me.
(subject)
Here are some pictures **(that)** we took on vacation.
(object)

Possessions (whose)
This is the new boy **whose** family has moved from the U.S.

Places (where)
That's the house **where** we lived a year ago.

Present perfect and simple past
Usage
- See Unit 1 for information about the usage and form of the simple past.
- We use the simple past, not the present perfect, when the past experience is finished or we add more information about a past experience.

Adverbs of time
- With the simple past, we use adverbs of time which show finished times in the past, such as *at three o'clock, in 2008, last night, on Saturday, yesterday, a week ago*.
- With the present perfect, we use adverbs of time which show unfinished times or a connection with the present, such as *already, ever, never, up to now, yet, so far*.
- Some adverbs of time can be used with the present perfect and the simple past, for example *this morning, recently*.

Restrictive adjective clauses
Usage
- We use restrictive adjective clauses starting with *who, that, whose,* or *where* to give essential information about the person, place or thing we are talking about.
- In conversation, we often replace *who* with *that*.

Form
- When *who* or *that* refers to the object, we can leave it out.
- You can't leave out *whose* or *where*.

Common mistakes
~~This is my friend fiancé you know already.~~ ✗
This is my friend whose fiancé you know already. ✓

Grammar practice

Present perfect with adverbs of time *ever, never, already, yet*

1 ★★ **Complete the sentences with the present perfect form of the verbs in parentheses.**

1 I *have* already *bought* (buy) a snack for my lunch.

2 Ian _____ (not take) the garbage out yet.

3 The children _____ never _____ (make) a mess in their bedroom!

4 Dad _____ already _____ (go) to the airport. His plane is leaving later this morning.

5 _____ the rain already _____ (start)?

6 We _____ (not spend) all our money yet.

7 _____ you _____ (find) your phone yet?

8 I _____ already _____ (be) to the library. Look, I have two books.

2 ★★ **Complete the telephone conversation with the present perfect form of the verbs in the box.**

> • clean • go (×2) • leave • look • make (×2)
> • not clean • not do • start

Amy: Hi, Tom. Are you busy?

Tom: Yes, I am. My dad **1** *has gone* to work and he **2** _____ a list of jobs for Katy and me. He wants us to do our homework, take the dog for a walk, clean our bedrooms, and make pizza for dinner! I don't know how to make pizza. **3** _____ you ever _____ one?

Amy: No, I haven't. Can Katy make the pizza?

Tom: No, she **4** _____ never _____ one before and she's a terrible cook.

Amy: **5** _____ you _____ the other jobs yet?

Tom: Yes, I **6** _____ already _____ my bedroom, but I **7** _____ my homework yet. Katy **8** _____ for a walk with the dog, but she **9** _____ her bedroom yet.

Amy: **10** _____ you _____ on the Internet for a pizza recipe?

Tom: No, I haven't but that's a good idea, thank you.

Present perfect and simple past

3 ★★ **Write sentences. Use the present perfect or the simple past with the time expression.**

1 I / come home / at eleven o'clock.
   I came home at eleven o'clock.

2 she / ever / win anything?
   _____

3 they / never / have a fight
   _____

4 he / not see / his girlfriend / yesterday
   _____

5 we / get along well / up to now
   _____

6 you / go out / with Alex / yet?
   _____

4 ★★ **Complete the text with the present perfect or the simple past form of the verbs in the box.**

> • be (×2) • get • invite • learn • make
> • move • not start • sit • ~~start~~

I **1** *started* this school four years ago and, so far, I **2** _____ with the same classmates. Last year I **3** _____ with a boy named Silvio but his family **4** _____ to Mexico. I **5** _____ an e-mail from him yesterday and he **6** _____ already _____ some Spanish. He **7** _____ school in Mexico yet but he **8** _____ already _____ friends in his neighborhood.

Silvio and his parents **9** _____ me to visit Mexico! I'm very excited because I **10** _____ never _____ to another country.

Restrictive adjective clauses with
who, that, whose, where

5 ★★ Complete what they are saying.

1 There's Don's wife *who* never cleans the house.
2 That's my daughter's fiancé _____ children
are living with his ex-wife.
3 Bill and his wife are living in a small apartment
_____ he lived when he was single.
4 My granddaughter is here with a boyfriend
_____ she met at a soccer game.
5 Fiona is wearing a dress _____ was very
expensive.
6 There are my two grandchildren _____ are
always noisy.

6 ★★ Join the sentences with the correct
adjective from the parentheses.

1 Jim is my uncle. He always sings at weddings.
(where/who) *Jim is my uncle who always sings at*
weddings.
2 That's my sister-in-law. Her parents live in Spain.
(that/whose) _____

3 That is the restaurant. My father asked my
stepmother to marry him. (where/who)

_____

4 This is the ring. My brother gave it to his fiancée.
(that/whose) _____

_____

5 I live with my dad, my stepmother and my
stepsister. They moved in last year.
(whose/who) _____

_____

Consolidation

7 Complete the interview with the correct form
of the verbs in parentheses. Use the present
perfect or the simple past.

Teacher: **1** *Have* you ever *thought* (think) about your
future?

Student: Yes, I have.

Teacher: **2** _____ you _____ (decide) what
job you want to do?

Student: I have some ideas but I **3** _____
(not decide) yet.

Teacher: What jobs **4** _____ you _____
(think) about?

Student: Well, last year I **5** _____ (want) to
be a farmer. Now I want to be a teacher.

Teacher: **6** _____ you _____ (spend) any
time with young children?

Student: Yes, I have. I have three younger sisters who
are all in elementary school. Two months
ago I **7** _____ (help) at their school
and I **8** _____ (enjoy) it.

Teacher: Good. **9** _____ you _____ (speak)
to your parents about your decision?

Student: Yes and no. My stepmother and I
10 _____ (talk) about it last night,
but I **11** _____ (not speak) to my
dad yet.

too + adjective + to

I am **too late to** catch the bus.
He/She/It's **too lazy to** pass the test.
You/We/They're **too serious to** enjoy parties.

(not) + adjective + enough to

I'm **(not) old enough to** drive.
He/She/It's **(not) fast enough to** finish the race first.
You/We/They're **(not) confident enough to** sing in a band.

too + adverb + to

I/You/We/They run **too slowly to** win a race.
He/She/It speaks **too quietly to** act in a play.

(not) + adverb + enough to

I/You/We/They speak French **well enough to** work in France.
I/You/We/They **don't** speak French **well enough to** work in France.
He/She/It thinks **quickly enough to** win the contest.
He/She/It **doesn't** think **quickly enough to** win the contest.

too many, too much, not enough

There are **too many** cars.   There is **too much** garbage.
There is**n't enough** information.   There are**n't enough** buses.

Indefinite pronouns *some-, any-, no-, every-* + thing, where, one, body

I have **something** in my eye.
Let's go **somewhere** hot for our vacation.
Someone/Somebody knows the answer.

He doesn't know **anything** about sports.
Can I go climbing **anywhere** in this town?
Does **anyone/anybody** know the answer?

Nothing ever happens here. It's so boring!
There's **nowhere** for young people to go on the weekends.
No one/Nobody answered the teacher's question.

Ask Annabelle. She knows **everything** about Seattle.
I looked **everywhere** for my phone.
I asked **everyone/everybody** in my class the question.

Notes

too + adjective/adverb + to; *(not) + adjective/adverb + enough to*

Usage

- We can make many adjectives and adverbs stronger or weaker by adding *too . . . to* or *(not) . . . enough to*.
  too = more than necessary
  (not) enough = (not) the right amount
- Someone can be more or less *smart*.
  He's smart.
  He isn't smart enough to be in this class.
- Someone can drive more or less *fast*.
  She's driving fast.
  She's driving too fast to stop.
- *very* and *too* mean different things.
  He's very tall = a fact.
  He's too tall = it's a problem.

too many, too much, not enough

Usage

We use

- *too many* with plural, count nouns.
- *too much* with non-count nouns.
- *not enough* with both count and non-count nouns.

Indefinite pronouns *some-, any-, no-, every-* + *thing, where, one, body*

Usage

We use

- *something, somewhere, someone/somebody* when the identity of the object, person, or place isn't known.
- *anything, anywhere, anyone/anybody* for unknown objects, places, and people in questions and negative sentences.
- *nothing, nowhere, no one/nobody* to mean the same as *not anything, not anywhere, not anyone/anybody.*
- *everything, everywhere, everyone/everybody* in positive sentences when we talk about all unidentified objects, people, or places.

Common mistakes

- We don't use *no- + thing, where, one, body* in negative sentences.

Grammar practice

too + adjective/adverb + *to*; (*not*) + adjective/adverb + *enough to*

1 ★ **Complete the conversations with the correct form of the adjectives and adverbs in parentheses.**

1 Can I walk to the nearest swimming pool?

No, it's ten miles away. It's <u>*too far to*</u> (far) walk there.

2 Mom, will you drive me to town, please?

No, I won't. It's _____ (difficult) park.

3 Let's take all our friends to the theater. How much are the tickets?

They're $100! They are _____ (expensive) take everyone.

4 Why are you taking a cab to the station?

Because the bus goes _____ (slowly) get me there on time.

5 Do you want to have lunch in that restaurant?

No, thanks. They _____ serve _____ (fast) have lunch in half an hour.

6 Why do you buy your clothes in that store?

Because they sell things _____ (cheaply) get something new every week.

2 ★★ **Write sentences. Use the prompts and the correct adjective or adverb from the box.**

• high • not long • quickly • quietly • well • wide

1 truck / go under the bridge

The truck is too tall to go
under the bridge.

2 car / fit in the parking space

_____
_____

3 bed / sleep in

_____
_____

4 walk / arrive on time

_____
_____

5 talk / be heard

_____
_____

6 sleep / be at school

_____
_____

4

too many, too much, not enough

3 ★ Write the second sentence. Choose a phrase from each box.

• There is • There are	• books in it. • bad news. • fresh air in here. • ~~people on the bus.~~ • players to make two teams. • pollution.
• not enough • too many • too much	

1 Let's walk.

  There are too many people on the bus.

2 I can't carry my school bag.

  _____

3 We can't play soccer.

  _____

4 I never read a newspaper.

  _____

5 You can't go running next to a busy street.

  _____

6 Please open the window.

  _____

4 ★★ Write two sentences about each piece of information. Use *too much/many* and *not enough*.

1 There are forty thousand cars and two hundred places to park.

  There are too many cars.

  There aren't enough places to park.

2 Every day, sixteen thousand people travel on the city's ten buses.

  _____

  _____

3 In the park there are two garbage cans. There is a ton of garbage every weekend.

  _____

  _____

4 Forty people are at the party. There are two sandwiches.

  _____

  _____

Indefinite pronouns *some-, any-, no-, every-* + *thing, where, one, body*

5 ★ Circle the correct choices.

My school trip to France

Last year I went to Paris with my class. We stayed in a cheap hostel ¹ _b_ in the city center. On the first night, my friends and I went for a walk. We didn't tell ² _____ we were going out because it was early. We had ³ _____ to eat in a café. When we left the café, we got lost. I asked for directions to the hostel but ⁴ _____ understood my French!

We walked for about half an hour but ⁵ _____ looked strange. Then we sent text messages to our classmates but ⁶ _____ knew where we were. We found the hostel at ten o'clock and our teachers were very angry with ⁷ _____ in our group.

The next day we went ⁸ _____ in a big group. At the Eiffel Tower someone said ⁹ _____ to me in French but I didn't understand so I didn't say ¹⁰ _____ .

On the last day, I lost my passport. I looked ¹¹ _____ for it but I couldn't find it. In the end somebody found it under their bed!

1 a) anywhere   (b) somewhere)   c) everywhere
2 a) someone   b) anyone   c) nobody
3 a) anything   b) everything   c) something
4 a) no one   b) anybody   b) anyone
5 a) everything b) anywhere   c) somewhere
6 a) everyone   b) no one   c) anyone
7 a) someone   b) anyone   c) everybody
8 a) anywhere   b) nowhere   c) everywhere
9 a) nothing   b) anything   c) something
10 a) anything   b) something   c) nothing
11 a) nowhere   b) somewhere   c) everywhere

6 ★★ Replace the underlined words with a pronoun. Make any other changes necessary.

1 Alice enjoyed <u>the famous places, the theaters and the shops</u> in Seattle.

Alice enjoyed everything in Seattle.

2 Do you want <u>tea, coffee, soda, or water</u> to drink?

_____

_____

3 <u>A person in the street</u> gave me directions to the station.

_____

_____

4 Is there <u>a restaurant or café where</u> I can get a meal?

_____

_____

5 Do <u>Ethan, Jane, Amber, or Leo</u> know the way to the park?

_____

_____

6 <u>All the students in my class</u> are going to the library after school.

_____

_____

7 My dad put <u>all the things for our vacation</u> in the car.

_____

_____

8 When my parents visited Naples, they walked <u>to all the different places in the city</u>.

_____

_____

9 Luckily, we found <u>a place in a street</u> to park.

_____

_____

10 I'm very hungry and I don't have <u>a snack, a sandwich, or any fruit</u> to eat.

_____

_____

11 At our local swimming pool there is<u>n't a place</u> to buy a snack.

_____

_____

Consolidation

7 Complete the text.

Southtoft is a very small town next to the ocean. Visitors love it because there is a pretty beach and there are lots of small stores and expensive restaurants. But not everyone in the town is happy.

One local told us, "In the summer it is **1** *too* busy *to* move! There **2** _____ tourists. There **3** _____ traffic and the town **4** _____ big _____ for all the cars. The stores sell things that are **5** _____ expensive _____ buy. Our little beach **6** _____ big _____ for hundreds of people."

The hotel owner said, "I like the summer but my hotel is **7** _____ small _____ have more than eight guests a night. In the winter, people **8** _____ visit often _____ for me to make any money."

A teenager said, "It's so boring! There's **9** _____ for young people here. In the summer, there **10** _____ old people and in the winter, it's really boring. I'm seventeen so I'm **11** _____ old _____ go to the youth club but I'm **12** _____ old _____ to drive to Ipsmouth where there are real clubs."

Present perfect with *for* and *since*

Affirmative

I/You/We/They**'ve known** Alice **for** ten years.
He/She/It**'s been** in the park **since** four o'clock.

Negative

I/You/We/They **haven't seen** Alice **since** last October.
He/She/It **hasn't made** a mistake **for** a week.

Questions   Short answers

Have they **been married**
for a long time?   Yes, they **have**.   No, they **haven't**.
Has he **spoken** to you
since last weekend?   Yes, he **has**.   No, he **hasn't**.

Wh- questions

Who **have** you **spoken** to **since** you arrived?
Where **has** she **been for** the last five months?

Present perfect continuous with *for* and *since*

Affirmative

I/You/We/They**'ve been looking** forward to the party **since** last weekend.
He/She/It**'s been sleeping** for two hours.

Negative

I/You/We/They **haven't been waiting** here **since** Sunday.
He/She/It **hasn't been listening for** the last ten minutes.

Questions   Short answers

Have you **been waiting**
since last night?   Yes, I **have**.   No, I **haven't**.
Has she **been standing**
outside **for** a long time? Yes, she **has**.   No, she **hasn't**.

Wh- questions

Why **have** I **been waiting** here **for** ten minutes?
How long **has** it **been sitting** there?

Notes

Present perfect

Usage and form See Unit 3.

Present perfect continuous

Usage

- We use the present perfect continuous
  - for an activity that started in the past and is still happening. *We've been waiting here since nine o'clock.* = We started waiting at nine o'clock and we're still waiting now.
  - for a continuous activity with results in the present. *She's been waiting for two days and now she is first in the line.* = She waited for a long time, now she is the first person in the line.
- We often use the present perfect continuous with *How long . . . ?*

Form

- To form the present perfect continuous we use the correct form of *have* + *been* + the gerund (*-ing* form) of the verb.

Present perfect and present perfect continuous with *for* and *since*

- We use the present perfect and present perfect continuous with *for* and *since* to show the duration of an action or event.
- We use *for* with a period of time up to the present: *for five minutes, for two years*.
- We use *since* to give the particular point of time in the past when the action started: *since 1965, since January*.

Present perfect or present perfect continuous?

- We use the present perfect to focus on actions or events completed at an unspecified time in the past: *He's eaten his dinner*. (It's finished.)
- We use the present perfect continuous to focus on actions or events continuing up to now, that have either only just stopped or are still happening: *He's been working since seven o'clock*. (He's still working.)

Grammar practice

Present perfect

1 ★ Put *for* or *since* in the correct places in the sentences.

since
1 I've lived in Seattle ∧ I started elementary school.
2 Denny Park has been a public park more than 100 years.
3 People have lived in the Pioneer Square district 1851.
4 There hasn't been a major fire in Seattle 1889.
5 Trains have connected Seattle with the rest of the U.S. over a century and a half.
6 The population in the city of Seattle hasn't changed much the middle of the 1900s.
7 The population in the suburbs of Seattle has grown a lot then.

2 ★★ Complete the sentences with the present perfect form of *make* or *do*.

1 This answer is wrong. You*'ve made* a mistake.
2 We _____ any shopping for a week so there's nothing in the fridge.
3 _____ you _____ a cup of a coffee for everyone?
4 Kathy _____ any exercise since she broke her leg.
5 Dan has worked hard for six months and it _____ a difference to his grades.
6 Don't worry—you _____ your best.
7 Why is Ellie tired? She _____ anything all day.
8 _____ Mom _____ breakfast this morning?

Present perfect continuous

3 ★★ Complete the conversation with the present perfect continuous form of the verbs in parentheses.

Al: Hi, Ben. How long **1** *have you been living* (you live) here in Tacoma?
Ben: I arrived in June so I **2** _____ (live) here for three months.
Al: What **3** _____ (you do)?
Ben: I **4** _____ (work) in a hotel since July because I need to save some money.
Al: Are you staying at the hotel?
Ben: No, I **5** _____ (stay) with my aunt.
Al: How **6** _____ that _____ (be)?
Ben: It's not great right now. She has some other guests this week so I **7** _____ (not sleep) in a bedroom, I **8** _____ (sleep) on her sofa.

4 ★★ Write questions and answers. Use the present perfect continuous form with *for* or *since*.

1 *How long have they been doing their homework? They've been doing their homework for an hour.*

2 _____
_____
_____
_____

3 _____
_____
_____
_____

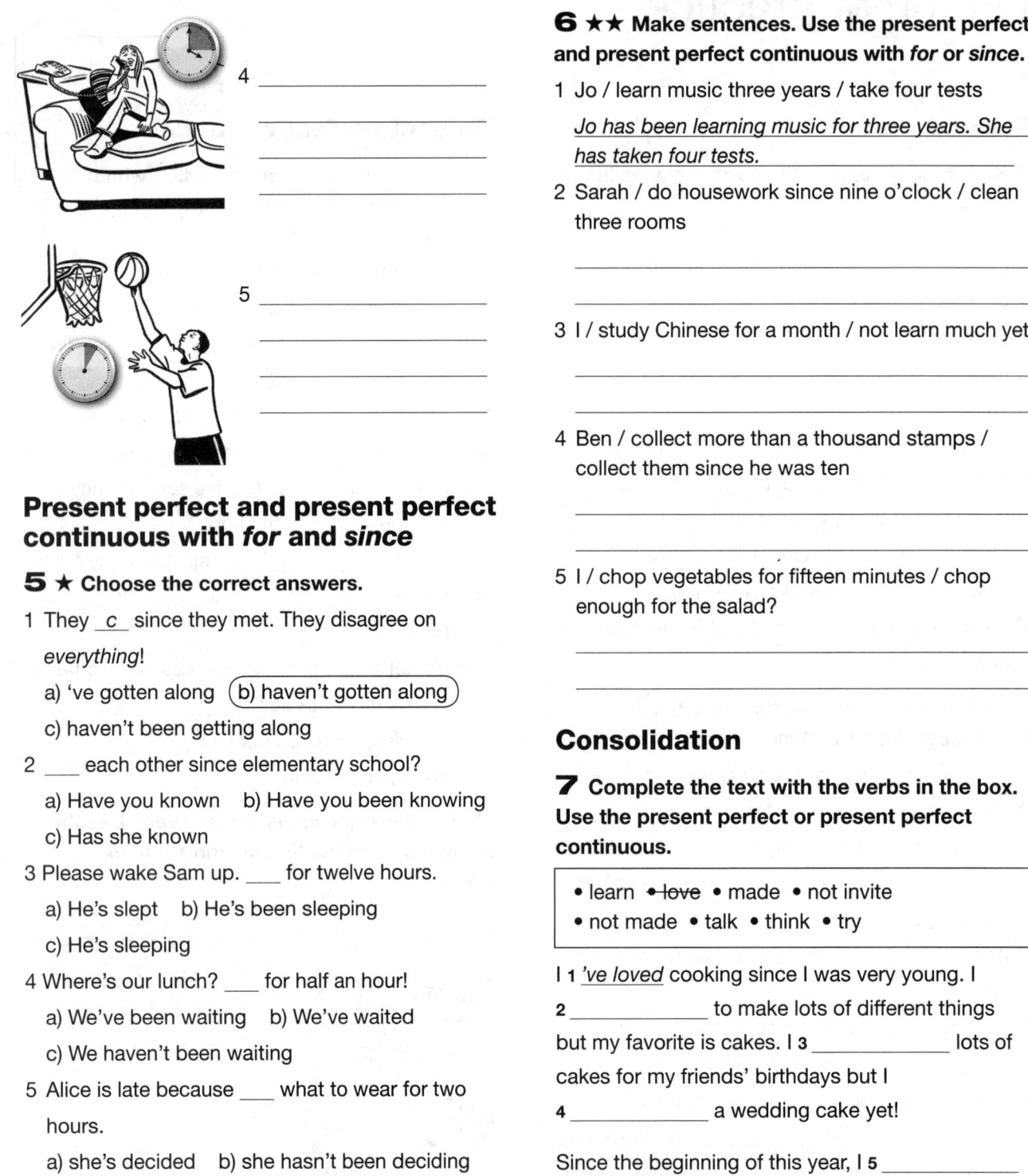

4 _____
_____
_____
_____

5 _____
_____
_____
_____

Present perfect and present perfect continuous with *for* and *since*

5 ★ Choose the correct answers.

1 They _c_ since they met. They disagree on *everything*!

   a) 've gotten along   (b) haven't gotten along)

   c) haven't been getting along

2 ____ each other since elementary school?

   a) Have you known   b) Have you been knowing

   c) Has she known

3 Please wake Sam up. ____ for twelve hours.

   a) He's slept   b) He's been sleeping

   c) He's sleeping

4 Where's our lunch? ____ for half an hour!

   a) We've been waiting   b) We've waited

   c) We haven't been waiting

5 Alice is late because ____ what to wear for two hours.

   a) she's decided   b) she hasn't been deciding

   c) she's been deciding

6 "The boys look tired. ____ ?"

   "Yes—for two hours!"

   a) Have they run   b) Has they been running

   c) Have they been running

6 ★★ Make sentences. Use the present perfect and present perfect continuous with *for* or *since*.

1 Jo / learn music three years / take four tests

   Jo has been learning music for three years. She has taken four tests.

2 Sarah / do housework since nine o'clock / clean three rooms

   _____

   _____

3 I / study Chinese for a month / not learn much yet

   _____

   _____

4 Ben / collect more than a thousand stamps / collect them since he was ten

   _____

   _____

5 I / chop vegetables for fifteen minutes / chop enough for the salad?

   _____

   _____

Consolidation

7 Complete the text with the verbs in the box. Use the present perfect or present perfect continuous.

| • learn • love • made • not invite |
| • not made • talk • think • try |

I **1** *'ve loved* cooking since I was very young. I **2** _____ to make lots of different things but my favorite is cakes. I **3** _____ lots of cakes for my friends' birthdays but I **4** _____ a wedding cake yet!

Since the beginning of this year, I **5** _____ food from different countries. I've made Chinese, Indian, and Japanese snacks. Friends ask, "Why **6** _____ you _____ us for a Chinese meal?"

Tonight, I'm cooking dinner with my friends David and Sally. I **7** _____ about what to cook all day. Sally **8** _____ about Middle Eastern food, so I'll make that!

used to

Affirmative
I/You/He/She/It/We/They **used to** sing in a band.

Negative
I/You/He/She/It/We/They **didn't use to** have long hair.

Questions	Short answers	
Did she **use to** wear a school uniform?	Yes, she **did**.	No, she **didn't**.

Wh- questions
Where **did** they **use to** live?

Notes

used to

Usage
- We only use *used to* for past habits or states which are no longer true.
  I used to ride a bike.
  (I don't ride a bike now.)
  I didn't use to have a car.
  (I have a car now.)

Form
- The form is the same for all persons.
- In affirmative sentences we use *used to* + the infinitive without *to*.
- In negative sentences we use *didn't* + *use to* + the infinitive without *to*.
- In questions, we use *did* + subject + *use to* + the infinitive without *to*.
- There is no present, perfect or continuous form of *used to*.

Common mistakes
- It is easy to confuse *used to* for past habits with the verb *to use*.
  He used to ride a motorcycle to gigs.
  (= past habit)
  He used a motorcycle to get to gigs.
  (= made use of, rode)

Past ability: *could* and *was/were able to*

Affirmative
I/You/He/She/It/We/They **could** climb mountains.
I/He/She/It **was able to** swim to the beach.
You/We/They **were able to** find some food.

Negative
I/You/He/She/It/We/They **couldn't** run a marathon.
I/He/She/It **wasn't able to** climb the tree.
You/We/They **weren't able to** find any water.

Questions / Short answers

Could she believe
the news? / Yes, she **could**. / No, she **couldn't**.
Was I **able to** walk
after the accident? / Yes, I **was**. / No, I **wasn't**.
Were you **able to** build
a house? / Yes, we **were**. / No, we **weren't**.

Wh- questions
What **could** I/you/he/she/it/we/they see?
How much **was** I/he/she/it **able to** carry?
How far **were** you/we/they **able to** jump?

Past perfect

Affirmative
I/You/He/She/It/We/They **had bought** a wallet.

Negative
I/You/He/She/It/We/They **hadn't forgotten** the tickets.

Questions / Short answers
Had you **identified** the woman? / Yes, I **had**. / No, I **hadn't**.

Wh- questions
Why **had** the police **asked** lots of questions?

Past ability: *could* and *was/were able to*

Usage
- We use the positive form of *could* or *was/were able to* for a general ability in the past.
- For a specific ability on one occasion, we use the positive form of *was/were able to*. We do not use *could*.
- We can use either *couldn't* or *wasn't/weren't able to* for both general inability and specific inability on one occasion in the past.

Form
- We use *could* + the infinitive without *to*.
- We use the correct past form of *to be* + *able to* + the infinitive without *to*.

Past perfect

Usage
- We use the past perfect for something that happened before another event in the past. It is often used with the simple past and the past continuous.
The man went to the police because he had lost his memory. = First he lost his memory, then he went to the police.
Reporters were waiting outside the police station because they had heard about the mystery man. = First they heard about the mystery man, then they waited outside the police station.

Form
- We form the past perfect with *had* + the past participle.
- The form is the same for all persons.

Common mistakes
- Remember we use the past perfect for an event that happens **before** another event in the past.
When the woman arrived the police had identified the man. = First the police identified the man, then the woman arrived.
When the woman arrived the police identified the man. = The woman arrived and then the police identified the man.

Grammar practice

used to

1 ★ **Write what the people used to do. Use the correct form of *used to*.**

1 I *didn't use to* have a car but now I have a Porsche and a Rolls Royce.

2 Bob _____ work hard but he's very lazy now.

3 What _____ your grandparents _____ do when they had jobs?

4 Lily _____ eat meat but now she only eats vegetables.

5 My mom _____ go to all-night parties but now she always goes to bed early.

6 Where _____ your dad _____ go to school?

7 Mike _____ do any exercise but now he goes to the gym every day.

2 ★★ **Complete the text with correct form of *used to* and the verbs in the box.**

> • do • get • go • not have • not ride
> • not watch • play • read • walk

When I was a child, we lived next to the ocean. In the summer, I **1** *used to go* swimming every day and in the winter my friends and I **2** _____ on the beach for hours. At night, we **3** _____ television because there weren't any cartoons or children's shows. We **4** _____ lots of books and tell stories. What did your grandparents **5** _____ in the evenings?

My parents **6** _____ a car so my mom used to walk to elementary school with me. When I was older, I **7** _____ with my friends. There was a lot of traffic so we **8** _____ our bicycles to school. How did you **9** _____ to elementary school?

Past ability: *could* and *was/were able to*

3 ★ **Choose the best choices. Write either *a*, *b*, or *a/b* if both choices are correct.**

1 When I was younger, I _a/b_ swim.
   a) couldn't   b) wasn't able to

2 On my sixth birthday I learned to swim. I _b_ put my face in the water the first time I tried.
   a) could   b) was able to

3 Teenagers didn't use to have cell phones. They ___ call each other and send texts all day and night!
   a) couldn't   b) weren't able to

4 My mother hasn't run in a marathon since college. She ___ run a seven-minute mile back then.
   a) could   b) was able to

5 ___ finish your homework before the game?
   a) Could you   b) Were you able to

6 Before the Thai restaurant on Broadway opened, you ___ get Thai food in this neighborhood.
   a) couldn't   b) weren't able to

7 ___ speak French before you moved to Paris?
   a) Could you   b) Were you able to

8 Longrun River used to be clean enough to eat the fish in it. My grandparents went fishing there one day on their honeymoon. They caught fresh fish during the day, and they ___ eat it at night.
   a) could   b) were able to

9 Yesterday John ___ do the laundry, clean his room, and take out the garbage . . . all before school!
   a) could   b) was able to

10) She tried calling him, but she ___ reach him.
   a) couldn't   b) wasn't able to

11) Michael Jordan ___ easily score thirty points a game when he played basketball.
   a) could   b) was able to

4 ★★ Complete the text with the correct form of *could* or *was/were able to* and the verbs in parentheses. Sometimes two answers are possible.

One night two weeks ago, I 1 *couldn't sleep* (not sleep) so I was reading in bed. Then, suddenly, I smelled smoke so I called the fire department from my bedroom. I woke up my family and we 2 _____ (escape) from the house.

Luckily, the fire engine arrived in three minutes. We 3 _____ (see) the fire upstairs but the firefighters 4 _____ (not see) how serious it was. They went into the house and fortunately they 5 _____ (put out) the fire very quickly.

We were very lucky. We 6 _____ (not live) in the house for a few days but the next weekend we 7 _____ (move) back.

Past perfect

5 ★ Complete the text with the past perfect form of the verbs in parentheses.

When Amy Howes got home from the college library, she saw that someone 1 *had been* (be) in her apartment. She 2 _____ (leave) dirty dishes in the kitchen after breakfast but now the kitchen was clean. She went into her bedroom. That morning she 3 _____ (not make) her bed and she 4 _____ (leave) lots of things on the floor. During the day, someone 5 _____ (make) her bed and 6 _____ (put) all her clothes away.

Amy was getting worried. She knew her roommate 7 _____ (not clean). 8 _____ a very neat burglar _____ (clean) the apartment? At that moment, she heard a sound in the living room. It was her older brother, Tom. He 9 _____ (find) the door unlocked so he 10 _____ (come in) and cleaned up.

6 ★★ Complete the sentences with the simple past or past perfect form of the verbs.

1 Our visitors *were* late because they *had lost* their way. (lose/be)

2 Mr. Jackson _____ his temper because the children _____ his car. (lose/paint)

3 Before my family _____ to France last month we _____ abroad. (go/not go)

4 Tom _____ an MP3 player until he _____ enough money. (can't buy/save)

5 How many people _____ before they _____ the right person? (the police interview/find)

6 I _____ anything in the test until I _____ everything. (not write/read)

7 How far _____ before it _____ raining? (you walk/start)

Consolidation

7 Choose the answers.

When my mom was a teenager she 1 _b_ in a small jazz band. She 2 ____ a good trumpet so she got a weekend job. After six months, she 3 ____ enough money and she 4 ____ buy a new trumpet.

Her dad 5 ____ the band to concerts but he 6 ____ because he hated jazz. He 7 ____ where his daughter's musical interests came from. He 8 ____ , "I can't stand listening to that terrible noise!" and my mom always replied "But I love it!"

1 a) use to played   (b) used to play)
   c) was able to play

2 a) hadn't afforded   b) couldn't afford
   c) didn't use to afford

3 a) could save   b) used to save   c) had saved

4 a) used to   b) could   c) was able to

5 a) used to drive   b) had driven   c) was driving

6 a) couldn't stay   b) didn't use to stay
   c) hadn't stayed

7 a) hadn't understood   b) wasn't understanding
   c) couldn't understand

8 a) use to say   b) used to said   c) used to say

Simple present passive

Affirmative
Suede **is made** from animals.
The shoes **are kept** in cardboard boxes.

Negative
Coffee **isn't grown** in Africa.
Silk clothes **aren't made** from plants.

Questions
Is cotton **made** from a plant?
Are the clothes **cleaned**?

Short answers
Yes, it **is**.   No, it **isn't**.
Yes, they **are**. No, they **aren't**.

Wh- questions
How much money **is** a worker **given**?

Simple past passive

Affirmative
This bag **was made** from recycled material.
The hats **were given** to the thrift shop.

Negative
The shop **wasn't run** by volunteers.
The bottles **weren't collected** from the recycling bin.

Questions
Was a new store **opened** last week?
Were the workers **supported** by Fairtrade?

Short answers
Yes, it **was**.   No, it **wasn't**.

Yes, they **were**. No, they **weren't**.

Wh- questions
Where **were** the plastic bottles **made**?

Nonrestrictive adjective clauses: *who, whose, which, where*

people (who)
Paula, **who** used to drive to school, now takes the bus.

possessions (whose)
The actor Ewan McGregor, **whose** movies include *Star Wars* and *Stormbreaker*, rode a motorcycle from the U.K. to South Africa.

things (which)
Ben Nevis, **which** is in Scotland, is the U.K.'s highest mountain.

places (where)
Niagara Falls, **where** 41 million gallons of water drop every minute, is between Canada and the U.S.

Notes
Present and past passive
Usage
- We use the passive to say what is/was done to a thing or person.
- We use the passive when
  - The action or the object is more important than the subject.
  In England, a lot of money is given to animal charities.
  - We don't know the subject.
  Second-hand clothes are given to the thrift shop.
  - We want to talk about a process.
  The clothes are checked and washed before they are sold.

Form
- We form the present and past passive with the correct form of *to be* + the past participle of the verb.
- If it is important to say who or what the agent (= subject) is/was, we use *by*.
  The clothes are checked by volunteers.
  The picture was painted by a famous artist.

Nonrestrictive adjective clauses: *who, whose, which, where*
Usage
- We use nonrestrictive adjective clauses starting with *who, whose, which,* and *where* to give extra information about the person, place or thing we are talking about.
- Usually a sentence still makes sense if you remove the clause.
  Kerry, which is in the west of Ireland, is a beautiful place for a vacation.
  Kerry is a beautiful place for a vacation.

Form
- A nonrestrictive clause is separated from the main information by a comma or, if it is in the middle of a sentence, two commas.
  They climbed to the top of the mountain, where they took some photographs.
  Peter Hillary, whose father climbed Everest fifty years before, climbed the mountain in 2003.

7 Grammar Practice

Simple present passive

1 ★★ Rewrite the sentences using the simple present passive.

1 They make suede from leather.
Suede is made from leather.

2 What do they make glass from?
_____

3 They don't open the store on Sunday.
_____

4 They don't give away plastic bags.
_____

5 They give old clothes to the store.
_____

6 Where do they keep all the clothes?
_____

7 They sell Fairtrade chocolate in the store.
_____

Simple past passive

2 ★★ Complete the text with the simple past passive form of the verbs in the box.

> • bring • create • make • pick up • sell
> • start (×2) • throw away

The popular shopping website eBay **1** *was started* in 1995 in California. It **2** _____ by a man named Pierre Omidyar. Buyers and sellers **3** _____ together by the website. People have bought lots of strange things on eBay. For example, a half-eaten sandwich **4** _____ for $500.

A similar website is Freecycle. The name **5** _____ from "free" and "recycle." Unlike eBay, it **6** _____ to give things away, not to sell them. A Freecycle user said, "I love it! In the past so many useful things **7** _____ . Last week, I advertised my children's old bikes and a few days later they **8** _____ by a young family."

Present and past passive

3 ★★ Complete the text with the present or past passive form of the verbs in parentheses.

The charity Oxfam **1** *was started* (start) in Oxford in 1942. The charity does work to help people all over the world and money **2** *is raised* (raise) in lots of different ways. However, one of the most successful ways they raise money is through their thrift stores.

Oxfam's first store **3** _____ (open) in Oxford in 1948. Lots of things **4** _____ (give) to this first store including plastic teeth and a house boat! In the following years, more stores **5** _____ (open) and now there are more than 750 in England and other countries.

Now, Oxfam also has about seventy bookstores where millions of second-hand books **6** _____ (sell) each year. A typical Oxfam bookstore **7** _____ (run) by about fifty volunteers. The books **8** _____ (bring) into the stores or they **9** _____ (leave) in "book banks". (A book bank is a large metal box in a public place like a parking lot.) Books which are very old or dirty **10** _____ (not sell) but the paper **11** _____ (recycle). Sometimes a very valuable book **12** _____ (find).
Recently, a very old Sherlock Holmes book **13** _____ (discover) in a store in Yorkshire and it **14** _____ (sell) for about $22,500!

Nonrestrictive adjective clauses:
who, whose, which, where

4 ★ **Complete the sentences with the nonrestrictive adjective clauses from the box.**

- where I got my dictionary
- which are all near the station
- ~~which are given to the store~~
- which is Fairtrade
- who loves cats and dogs
- whose names are in the news all the time

1 The clothes, *which are given to the store* , are sold to make money for a charity.

2 Penny Wilkins, _____ , is a volunteer working for an animal shelter.

3 The chocolate, _____ , is delicious.

4 The thrift stores, _____ , are great places to find interesting clothes.

5 The bookstore, _____ _____ , is having a sale next week.

6 Angelina Jolie and Brad Pitt, _____ _____ , gave more than $8 million to charity in 2006.

5 ★★ **Make sentences. Use relative pronouns.**

1 Bill Gates / one of the richest person in the world / left college before he got his degree
Bill Gates, who is one of the richest people in the world, left college before he got his degree.

2 Charles Babbage / was a nineteenth century scientist / designed the first computer
_____
_____

3 Silicon Valley / there are lots of computer companies / is in California
_____
_____

4 MP3 players / can hold hundreds of songs / are very small
_____
_____

5 Leonardo da Vinci / drawings included helicopters and small planes / lived nearly six hundred years ago
_____
_____

Consolidation

6 **Complete the information.**

In 1966, the World Cup **1** *was* stolen. Four months later, it **2** _____ found by a dog named Pickles. The cup, **3** _____ is made from gold, was wrapped in newspaper and hidden in a garden.

Van Gogh, **4** _____ paintings are some of the most famous in the world, sold only one painting when he was alive. Now, more than a hundred years after his death, his paintings **5** _____ sold for millions of dollars.

A lot of money **6** _____ raised when 97 second-hand books **7** _____ sold by Oxfam at a special sale. A copy of *Harry Potter and the Chamber of Secrets* **8** _____ sold for $600. However, a book by Rudyard Kipling, **9** _____ is one of England's best-known writers, **10** _____ bought by anyone.

Grammar Summary

will/won't/may/might for predictions

Affirmative
I/You/He/She/It/We/They **will/may/might go** on vacation.

Negative
I/You/He/She/It/We/They **won't/may not/might not get** cheap vacations in space.

Questions
Will/May/Might we **spend** more time abroad?

Short answers
Yes, we **will/may/might**.
No, they **won't/may not/might not**.

Wh- questions
When **will/may/might** tours to space **become** cheaper?

Conditional with *if/unless*

Affirmative
I/You/He/She/It/We/They **will be** nervous **if** the teacher **is** impatient.
I/You/He/She/It/We/They **will enjoy** camping **unless** it **rains** all the time.

Negative
I/You/He/She/It/We/They **won't learn** a lot **if** the teacher **is** inexperienced.
I/You/He/She/It/We/They **won't do** the indoor obstacle course **unless** it**'s** raining.

Questions
Will we **go** hiking **if** it**'s** snowing?

Short answers
Yes, we **will**.   No, we **won't**.

Wh- questions
Why **will** they **need** ropes **if** they **go** climbing?
How **will** I **get** there **unless** I **go** by car?

Notes
will/won't/may/might for predictions
Usage
- We use the modal auxiliaries *will/won't/may/might* to show how sure we are about future predictions.
- We use *will/won't* for predictions we are certain about.
  More people will fly. Vacations won't be more expensive.
- We use *may (not)* and *might (not)* for predictions we are not certain about.
  People may travel less. It might not be possible to have a vacation in space.

Form
- The main verb is the same for all persons.
- We use subject + *will/won't/may/might* + infinitive without *to*.

Conditional with *if/unless*
Usage
- We use the conditional with the conjunctions *if* and *unless* to talk about something that may happen in the future, as a result of something else happening.
- We use *if* for the result of an action happening.
  We'll arrive on time if we leave early.
- We use *unless* for the result of an action not happening.
  We'll be late unless we leave early.

Form
- There are two parts in a conditional sentence. We use *if/unless* + the simple present for the condition. We use *will* + the infinitive without *to* for the result. The two clauses are separated by a comma. The two clauses can be written in the reverse order without a comma.
  If you work harder, you'll get better grades.
  You will get better grades if you work harder.
  Unless you save some money, you won't get a new bicycle.
  You won't get a new bicycle unless you save some money.
- A conditional sentence can combine affirmative and negative clauses.

Future time clauses with *when/as soon as*

Affirmative
I **will call when/as soon as I get** to the station.

Negative
We **won't go** on vacation **when/as soon as** the term **ends**.

Questions
Will they **put up** the tent **when/as soon as** they **arrive**?

Short answers
Yes, they **will**.
No, they **won't**.

Wh- questions
Why **will** you **leave when/as soon as** it **gets** dark?

will with *when/as soon as*
Usage
- We use *will* with *when/as soon as* to show that
  - two future events will happen at almost the same time or one immediately after the other:
  They'll open the door when/as soon as we arrive.
  - one thing will happen very quickly after the other
  We'll put up our tent when/as soon as the rain stops.

Form
- There are two parts in a sentence with *will* + *when/as soon as*. We use *will* + the infinitive without *to* for the result. We use *when/as soon as* + the simple present for what must happen first. The two parts of the sentence can be in either order. If the *when/as soon as* clause is first, we use a comma.
I'll watch television as soon as I have finished my homework.
As soon as I have finished my homework, I'll watch television.
- The *will* clause can be positive or negative, the *when/as soon as* clause is usually positive.

Grammar Practice

will/won't/may/might for predictions

1 ★ Write predictions with *will, won't, may* or *may not*.

1 we / learn to dive (possible)

*We may learn to dive.*_____

2 they / not go climbing (definite)

_____

3 we / travel by car (definite)

_____

4 she / not stay in a hotel (possible)

_____

5 the flight / leave late (possible)

_____

2 ★★ Complete the text. Use the verbs in the box with *will, won't, might* or *might not*.

> • fly (definite) • ~~go (definite)~~ • look for (possible)
> • not drive (definite) • not stay (definite)
> • take (possible) • visit (possible) • not visit (definite)

I've decided that I **1** *'ll go* to Florida for my vacation.
It's a very long trip so I **2** _____ , I
3 _____ . I definitely **4** _____ Miami
because it's too big. I **5** _____ Orlando or
Tampa but I haven't decided yet. I **6** _____ in
hotels because they are very expensive. I
7 _____ a tent or I **8** _____ a hostel.

Conditional with *if/unless*

3 ★ Complete the conditional sentences with *if, unless, will,* or *won't*.

1 *Unless* we run, we won't catch the train.

2 I _____ go on vacation unless you pay for me.

3 _____ you have a passport, they won't let
you on the plane.

4 We will camp on the beach _____ we don't
have enough money for a hostel.

5 If the food's bad, we _____ buy sandwiches
and eat in our hotel room.

4 ★★ Complete the second sentence so it means the same as the first.

1 We'll stay at home if it rains.

We'll stay at home unless it's sunny.

2 Unless it's cheap, we won't have lunch in the café.

If it's cheap, _____ .

3 I'll call you if I'm late.

_____ I'm on time.

4 We'll sleep in the tent if there isn't a hotel.

We won't sleep in the tent _____

_____ .

5 You will have to practice on the climbing wall if
you haven't climbed before.

If you have climbed before, _____

_____ .

6 Unless the people are friendly, it will be boring.

It'll be fun _____ .

will with *when/as soon as*

5 ★ Join the sentences with *when* or *as soon as*.

1 I'll get home. I'll make a sandwich. (when)

*When I get home, I'll make a sandwich.*_____

2 I'll get a new computer. I'll download lots of
music. (as soon as)

_____

_____

3 I'll finish my homework. I'll play chess with you.
(as soon as)

_____

_____

4 You'll show your parents your grades. They'll be
pleased. (when)

_____

_____

5 Nell will earn some money. She'll buy a
saxophone. (when)

_____

_____

6 ★★ Write *will* sentences with *when* or *as soon as*.

1 she arrive / go to her pen pal's home

When she arrives, she'll go to her pen pal's home.

2 she find a language school / her pen pal goes back to school

_____

_____

3 she get a job in a beach café / finish the language class

_____

_____

4 the café close for the winter / she go to Portugal

_____

_____

Consolidation

7 Complete the conversation.

In the morning

Oliver: Will you help me get ready for my camping trip, Mom?

Mrs. Davis: OK. 1 _If_ you write a list of everything you need to do, I 2 _____ help you.

Oliver: Thanks. I'll start the list 3 _____ I get home this evening.

That evening

Mrs. Davis: Have you made your list yet?

Oliver: Yes, I've started it. Do you want to see it?

Mrs. Davis: No, thanks. I'll look at it 4 _____ I finish cooking.

Oliver: Can I read it to you?

Mrs. Davis: No, don't do that. 5 _____ I read it, I won't remember anything.

Oliver: OK. How long will you be?

Mrs. Davis: 6 _____ you help me do the vegetables, I 7 _____ be quicker.

Oliver: I don't mind helping. What do you want me to do?

Mrs. Davis: 8 _____ you chop the onions, I 9 _____ peel the potatoes.

Oliver: Oh, no, I'll start crying 10 _____ I cut the first onion!

Mrs. Davis: If you put the onions in the freezer for ten minutes, you 11 _____ cry.

Oliver: Is that true?

Mrs. Davis: Yes, it is.

Grammar Summary

Reported requests and commands

Direct request
"Can you **open** the window, please?"

Reported request
She **asked me to open** the window.

Direct command
"**Open** your books!"

Reported command
Our teacher **told us to open** our books.

Reported statements

Direct statement
"I **love** my job."

"**I'm feeling** better."

"We **ran** to school."

"It**'s rained** for three days."

"**I'll** help you."

"I **can** see you later."

Reported statement
He **said (that) he loved** his job.

She **said (that) she was feeling** better.

They **told me (that) they had run** to school.

He **said (that) it had rained** for three days.

She **told me (that) she would** help me.

He **said that he could** see me later.

Reported questions

Wh- questions

Direct question
"**Where do** you **live**?"

"**Why is** Ted late?"

Reported question
He **asked (me) where** I **lived**.

She **asked (me) why** Ted **was** late.

Yes/No questions

Direct question
"**Will** you go to the store?"

"**Can** you buy some cheese, please?"

"**Do** you **have** any money?"

Reported question
He **asked (me) if** I **would** go to the store.

She **asked (me) if** I **could** buy some cheese.

He **asked (me) if** I **had** any money.

Notes

Reported requests and commands

Usage

• We use reported requests and commands to report what someone asked or told another person to do.

• We use *ask* in requests and *tell* in commands.

Form

• To report a polite request, we use subject + *asked* + object + infinitive.

• To report a command, we use subject + *told* + object + infinitive.

Reported statements and questions

Form

• When we change a direct statement/question to a reported statement/question we make some changes to the structure.

  - We move the tense "back".
    simple present   → simple past
    present continuous → past continuous
    simple past   → past perfect
    present perfect   → past perfect
    will/can/may   → *would/could/might*

  - We usually change pronouns.
    "**I'm** Spanish." → *She said (that)* **she** *was Spanish*.

  - We usually change possessive adjectives.
    "That's **my** bag." → *He told us (that) it was* **his** *bag*.

  - We usually change time and place references.
    "I saw him **yesterday**." → *She told us (that) she had seen him* **the day before**.
    "I live **here**." → *He said he lived* **there**.

• We use an object noun or pronoun with *tell*. *He told* **us** *that there had been an accident*.

• If we want to say who the object is with *said*, we use *to* + name. *She* **said to Kathy** *that she was going to work*.

• With *say* and *tell*, we don't usually use *that* in informal writing and speech.

• In *Wh-* questions, we use *asked* + (object) + question word + subject + verb.

• In *Yes/No* questions, we use *asked* + (object) + *if* + subject + verb.

• We don't use a question mark.

Grammar Practice

Reported requests and commands

1 ★ Complete the reported requests and commands with the correct verbs and pronouns.

1 Gina said, "Could you carry my bag, please?"

Gina _asked_ me to carry _her_ bag.

2 Dan said, "Don't use my phone!"

Dan _____ his brother not to use _____ phone.

3 Mr. Simmonds said, "Children, please put your toys in the box."

Mr. Simmonds _____ the children to put _____ toys in the box.

4 Ben said, "Mom, could you pass me the butter, please?"

Ben _____ his mom to pass _____ the butter.

5 Mrs. Elliot said, "Tom, clean up your room!"

Mrs. Elliot _____ Tom to clean up _____ room.

6 Mr. Adams said, "Maria, can you move your car, please?"

Mr. Adams _____ Maria to move _____ car.

2 ★★ Write the conversations.

1 Henry asked his sister, Anna, to make his bed. She told him to do it himself.

Henry: _Please make my bed, Anna._

Anna: _Do it yourself!_

2 The teacher told the students to open their books to page 81. A student asked the teacher to say the page number again.

Teacher: _____

_____

Student: _____

_____

3 Mrs. Jenkins asked her son, Mike, to buy some vegetables. He asked her to make a shopping list for him.

Mrs. Jenkins: _____

_____

Mike Jenkins: _____

_____

4 Olivia asked her brother, Al, to help her with her homework. Al told Olivia to ask him again later.

Olivia: _____

_____

Al: _____

_____

5 The radio show told listeners to watch the sky for UFOs. A listener called and asked them to explain what "UFO" means.

Radio show: _____

_____

Listener: _____

_____

6 Mr. Daniels asked his son, Peter, to buy some blue cheese. Peter asked him to choose another cheese.

Mr. Daniels: _____

_____

Peter Daniels: _____

_____

Reported statements

3 ★★ Complete the reported speech.

1 "I live on Fulton Street."

She told him that _she lived on Fulton Street._

2 "We're looking for the swimming pool."

He said that _____

_____

3 "I'll help you do your homework."

She told Jane that _____

_____

4 "Diane went to the movies last night."

He said that _____

_____

5 "You can't go home until four o'clock."

The teacher said that the students _____

_____

4 ★★ **Read the police statement about a missing person. Complete the reported speech.**

"We are looking for Miss Harris, a twenty-year-old woman. She left her home on January 5 and caught the bus, but she never arrived at work. She will be easy to recognize because she is six feet tall with very long blond hair. You can see pictures of Miss Harris on the police website."

The police officer **1** *told* the reporters **2** *that they were looking for* Miss Harris, a twenty-year-old woman. The police officer then **3** _____ the reporters **4** _____ because she is six feet tall with very long blond hair. The police officer **5** _____ they **6** _____ of Miss Harris on the police website.

Reported questions

5 ★★ **Match the pictures (1–3) with the direct questions (a–c). Write the reported questions.**

a) "When did you pass your driving test?"
b) "Which road goes to Cambridge?"
c) "Will you marry me?"

1 _____

2 _____

3 _____

6 ★★ **Write the reported questions.**

1 "Nina, do you like dancing?"

I asked *Nina if she liked dancing.*

2 "Have Mark and Eve been to China?"

I asked _____

3 "Can Jay speak French?"

I asked _____

4 "How much is a dictionary, please?"

I asked _____

5 "Do Liam and his brother go to the same school?"

I asked _____

Consolidation

7 **Choose the correct answers.**

Will: Did you speak to Hannah's friend at the party?

Sarah: Yes, she told me about life in New York.

Will: New York? She **1** _c_ me that she lived in Paris.

Sarah: No, she definitely **2** ____ that she had an apartment in New York and that **3** ____ for an international bank.

Will: That's strange. She told me **4** ____ . She said **5** ____ in China for a year in 2009.

Sarah: Really? When we spoke, she said **6** ____ in Europe in 2009!

Will: I think she was lying.

Sarah: So do I!

1 a) asked   b) said   (c) told)

2 a) asked   b) said   c) told

3 a) I work   b) I worked   c) she worked

4 a) she was an engineer   b) I'm an engineer
   c) was an engineer

5 a) she has worked   b) she had worked
   c) I have worked

6 a) she has been working   b) I was working
   c) she was working

Conditional: *if* clause + *would*

Affirmative
I/You/He/She/It/We/They **would call** the police **if** there **was** an accident.
If the fire alarm **rang**, I/you/he/she/it/we/they **would leave** the building.

Negative
I/You/He/She/It/We/They **wouldn't scream if** a snake **came** in the room.
If the fire alarm **rang**, I/you/he/she/it/we/they **wouldn't panic**.

Questions	Short answers
Would she **tell** a lie **if** a friend **was** in trouble?	Yes, she **would**. No, she **wouldn't**.

Wh- questions
What **would** you **do if** you **won** a lot of money?

Wish with simple past clause

Affirmative
I/You/We/They **wish** it **was** their vacation.
He/She/It **wishes** it **was** sunny today.

Negative
I/You/We/They **wish** there **weren't** any tests this week.
He/She/It **wishes** the swimming pool **wasn't** closed.

Questions	Short answers	
Do I **wish** I **had** a lot of money?	Yes, I **do**.	No, I **don't**.
Does he **wish** it **was** the weekend?	Yes, he **does**.	No, he **doesn't**.

Wh- questions
Why **do** you **wish** you **were** a rock star?

Notes
Conditional: *if* clause + *would*
Usage
- We use the conditional for unlikely or impossible situations
  - in the present.
    They'd have motorcycles if they were older.
  - in the future.
    If I was asked to play Real Madrid tomorrow, I'd be amazed.

Form
- There are two parts in a conditional sentence.
  - We use *if* + the simple past for the unlikely or impossible condition.
  - We use *would* + the infinitive without *to* for the result.
- We can combine affirmative and negative clauses in a conditional sentence.
- We can put the two clauses in either order. When the *if* (condition) clause is first, we need a comma between it and the *would* (result) clause.

be in the conditional
- In informal written or spoken language we use *I/he/she/it was*.
  If I was an Olympic athlete, I'd be a swimmer.
- In formal written and spoken language, we sometimes use *I/he/she/it were*.
  If the president were here, I'd ask about climate change.

Wish with simple past clause
Usage
- We use this verb pattern to talk about present wishes and regrets when the wish/regret is unlikely or impossible.

Form
- We form the verb phrase with subject + *wish* + subject + simple past .

Common mistakes
- Don't confuse *wish* and *hope*.
  Wish means something you want to be true but you know is impossible or unlikely.
  Hope means you want something to be true and it's possible.

Conditional: *if* clause + *would*

1 ★★ Write the correct form of the verbs in parentheses. Use *would* where necessary.

1 If I *was* (be) alone at night, I *would be* (be) frightened.

2 If I _____ (see) a robbery, I _____ (call) the police.

3 I _____ (not tell) someone if I _____ (not like) them.

4 My sister _____ (be) angry if I _____ (wear) her clothes.

5 I _____ (get) a new computer if I _____ (have) enough money.

6 If you _____ (find) a lot of money, what _____ you _____ (do)?

7 My mom _____ (not be) angry with me if I _____ (tell) the truth.

8 What _____ your parents _____ (say) if you _____ (not pass) the test?

9 If you _____ (win) a vacation, where _____ you _____ (go)?

10 My friend _____ (keep) a secret if I _____ (ask) her to.

2 ★★ Write the conversations. Use the conditional.

1 A: what you do / you not have to go to school?

   B: I stay in bed all morning / and I play basketball in the afternoon.

   A: *What would you do if you didn't have to go to school?*

   B: *I'd stay in bed all morning and I'd play basketball in the afternoon.*

2 C: you go anywhere / you go to Australia?

   D: no / I go to Peru.

   C: _____

   _____

   D: _____

3 E: how you feel / you see an elephant in the middle of Seattle?

   F: surprised!

   E: _____

   _____

   F: _____

4 G: you be nervous / you have to travel abroad alone?

   H: yes

   G: _____

   _____

   H: _____

5 J: what you do / your friend break your camera?

   K: I not worry / it be an accident

   J: _____

   _____

   K: _____

6 L: you be invited to a friend's party / you wear fancy clothes?

   M: no, not wear fancy clothes / I wear jeans

   L: _____

   _____

   M: _____

Wish with simple past clause

3 ★ Write sentences with *I wish*.

1 I don't speak Italian.

   I wish I spoke Italian.

2 I share a bedroom.

   _____

3 I can't drive.

   _____

4 I'm not going on vacation this year.

   _____

5 I argue with my sister.

   _____

6 I don't have many friends.

   _____

4 ★★ **Read the page from George's calendar. Write what he says with *I wish*.**

> I have lots to do today. Mom wants me to help her make dinner and Dad says I have to clean my bedroom. I can't go outside because the weather is terrible. I have some homework to do but I don't understand the math and I can't find my history book. My computer is broken so I can't use the Internet.

1 "*I wish I didn't have* lots to do today."

2 "_____ Mom _____ ."

3 "_____ clean my bedroom."

4 "_____ terrible."

5 "_____ my math homework."

6 "_____ my history book."

7 "_____ my computer _____ ."

Consolidation

5 **Write what the people are thinking. Use the conditional or *wish* with the simple past.**

- buy that car / rich • famous / not at school • fire / shout "help" and press the fire alarm button
- I can dance • I can have this pair • it not rain

1 *If there was a fire, I'd shout "help" and press the fire alarm button.*

Those are too expensive. How about these?

2 _____

3 _____

4 _____

5 _____

6 _____

Grammar Summary

so + adjective . . . (that) . . .

My computer's **so old (that)** it uses floppy disks.

such (a/an) + adjective + noun (that) . . .

It is **such a hot day that** we can't go jogging.
It was **such an awful hotel** that we moved.

Verb with infinitive

I **managed to do** all my homework last night.
She **hopes to see** her friends tomorrow.
They**'ve promised to help** us.
We **didn't agree to meet** at three o'clock.
Verbs which can be followed by the infinitive include:
afford, agree, arrange, ask, decide, expect, help, hope, learn, manage, offer, promise, refuse, seem, and *want.*

Verb with gerund

I **avoid flying**.
He **can't stand dancing**.
They **have denied downloading** the movies.
My grandparents **won't give up smoking**.
Verbs that can be followed by the gerund include:
admit, avoid, can't stand, delay, deny, enjoy, feel like, finish, give up, imagine, not mind, miss, practice, suggest, and *understand.*

Auxiliary verbs with so and neither

Affirmative	Agree	Disagree
I like swimming.	So do I.	I don't.
We're hungry.	So am I.	I'm not.
He's already eaten.	So have I.	I haven't.
They were bored by the movie.	So was I.	I wasn't.

Negative	Agree	Disagree
I don't enjoy dancing.	Neither do I.	I do.
She's not doing a lot of exercise at the moment.	Neither am I.	I am.
He hasn't bought a ticket yet.	Neither have I.	I have.
They can't climb over that wall.	Neither can I.	I can.

Notes

so + adjective . . . (that) . . . ; such (a/an) + adjective + noun (that) . . .

Usage
- We use *so* and *such (a/an)* to emphasize adjectives.
- We use *so* + adjective (*that*) and *such (a/an)* + adjective + noun (*that*) to show cause and effect.

Verb with infinitive; Verb with gerund

Usage
- We use the infinitive after some verbs (but not auxiliaries).
- We use a gerund (*-ing* form) after some verbs. We do this when we are using the gerund as a noun.
- We can use either the infinitive or the gerund with some verbs. These include: *allow, begin, forget, hate, like, love, prefer, regret, remember, start, stop,* and *try.*

Auxiliary verbs with so/neither

Usage
We use *so/neither* to express agreement.
- We use *so* to agree with an affirmative statement.
- We use *neither* to agree with a negative statement.

Form
- We use *so/neither* + auxiliary + subject to agree with a statement.
- We use subject + positive or negative form of the auxiliary to disagree with a statement.
- Both structures are used to reply to the sentence before so we repeat the tense and the auxiliary verb in the appropriate form.

Common mistakes
- We don't usually use a full verb with *so/neither* + auxiliary + subject.
  "So could I." ✓ *"So could I swim."* X
- We use *neither* to agree with a negative statement so we don't need another negative in the reply.
  "Neither did we." ✓ *"Neither didn't we."* X

Grammar Practice

Grammar Practice

Grammar Practice

so + adjective . . . (that) . . .; such (a/an) + adjective + noun (that) . . .

1 ★ Complete the sentences with so or such.

1. The robber was <u>so</u> stupid that he wrote his name on the wall.
2. It was _____ a serious crime that the police canceled all their vacations.
3. The burglars were _____ quiet that no one woke up.
4. The graffiti was _____ good that they decided not to clean the walls.
5. The vandal had to pay _____ a large fine that she went to prison instead.
6. The burglar's bag was _____ heavy that he couldn't carry it.

2 ★★ Write sentences. Use the simple past with so or such.

1. the prison food bad / the prisoners not want it
   The prison food was so bad that the prisoners didn't want it.
2. the bank robbers drive fast car / the police not catch them

3. the photo on the security camera good / the police identify the robbers quickly

4. the burglars take heavy things / they cannot carry them all

5. the witness take good photo with her phone / the newspapers used it

6. the burglar thin / she climb through the smallest window

Verb with infinitive; Verb with gerund

3 ★ Complete the sentences with the correct form of the verbs in parentheses.

1. Jake's mom refused *to let* (let) him take her laptop to school.
2. Liz expects _____ (get) good grades on her technology exam.
3. The man in the store suggested _____ (burn) a back-up CD.
4. Did you manage _____ (download) the movie?
5. My computer just decided _____ (crash)!
6. I promised _____ (show) my grandfather how to download music.
7. My parents enjoy _____ (go) to music stores so they never buy online.

4 ★★ Complete the e-mail with the correct form of the verbs in the box.

- buy • download • look • pay (×2)
- ~~sell~~ • shop • stop

From: Melissa
To: Angie

Hi Angie,

I have decided ¹*to sell* my old computer and get a new one. As you know, I can't stand ² _____ at computer stores so I hope ³ _____ something online. I don't mind ⁴ _____ a bit more if I can get something good. Which websites do you suggest ⁵ _____ at?

I recently managed ⁶ _____ some music from the Internet for the first time. (Of course I paid for it!) Until recently the boys refused ⁷ _____ for their music. However, their father and I explained that it is illegal and they promised ⁸ _____ .

Write soon!

Lots of love,

Melissa

Auxiliary verbs with *so* and *neither*

5 ★ **Complete the conversation with the sentences in the box.**

> • I do! • I have. • I won't. • Neither do I.
> • ~~So am I.~~ • So do I.

Chelsea: I'm very thirsty.

Brooklyn: 1 *So am I.* I like the café near the station.

Chelsea: 2 _____ Should we go there?

Brooklyn: Yes. I think I'll have a coffee and a burger.

Chelsea: 3 _____ I don't like meat.

Brooklyn: 4 _____ I love a good burger.

Chelsea: I haven't eaten a burger for two years.

Brooklyn: 5 _____ I usually have one on the weekend. But I don't like hotdogs.

Chelsea: 6 _____ They're gross!

6 ★★ **Complete the short conversations.**

(1) I read about the robbery in the newspaper. — _So_ did I.

(2) I saw the police arrest the vandal. — ____ didn't.

(3) I've never had my own computer. — ____ have I.

(4) I download movies from the Internet. — ____ because my computer is too old and very slow.

(5) I can't use my mom's credit card to buy things online. — ____ can I.

Consolidation

7 **Choose the correct answers.**

Lily: Can you help me carry these bags, please? I bought 1 ___b___ I can't carry them all.

Simon: Of course. Are you hungry? I had 2 _____ I'll need to eat something soon.

Lily: 3 _____ How about Gino's for a pizza?

Simon: I'm not sure. It's always 4 _____ that it takes about an hour. I can't stand 5 _____ when I'm hungry.

Lily: 6 _____ but everywhere is busy at lunchtime. I suggest 7 _____ a sandwich now and eating a bigger meal later.

Simon: OK. I like the Internet café in the mall.

Lily: 8 _____ Let's go there.

Simon: Good. Then I can check my e-mail. Do you want 9 _____ yours?

Lily: No, I'll enjoy 10 _____ them later.

Simon: OK. Let's go!

1 a) so heavy that (b) such heavy books that) c) the heaviest books

2 a) so small breakfast b) so hungry that c) such an early breakfast that

3 a) So do I. b) Neither do I. c) So will I.

4 a) such a quick place b) so busy c) so quick

5 a) wait b) waiting c) to wait

6 a) So can't I b) So am I c) Neither can I

7 a) getting b) get c) to get

8 a) Neither do I. b) So do I. c) So will I.

9 a) to check b) check c) checking

10 a) to read b) read c) reading

Rules and obligation: *must/have to*

Obligation
Present

I/You/He/She/It/We/They **must finish** the homework this evening.

I/You/He/She/It/We/They **can't (must not) drive** too fast.

I/You/We/They **have to go** to the dentist.

He/She/It **has to do** homework this evening.

Past

I/You/He/She/It/We/They **had to be** at school before eight o'clock.

No obligation
Present

I/You/We/They **don't have to** wear white clothes to play tennis.

He/She/It **doesn't have to practice** every day.

Past

I/You/He/She/It/We/They **didn't have to buy** expensive sports equipment.

Notes
Rules and obligation: *must/have to*

Usage
- We use *must/can't/must not* for written rules.
- We use *must/have to* for obligations.
- In affirmative sentences we use *must* and *have to*:
  - to talk about obligations that come from the speaker.
    I must go to bed early tonight. (= I'm tired, it's important to go to bed early.)
    Iris has to get a driver's license as soon as she's seventeen. (= The speaker thinks it's important for Iris to get a license.)
  - for obligations from other people.
    I have to go to bed before eleven o'clock on school nights (= It's my parent's rule.)
    You must be 16 years old to drive in Washington. (= It's the law.)
- We only use can't/*must not* for things you aren't allowed to do and with negative obligations. Must not is very formal.
  You can't play soccer on the grass.
  (= It's a park rule.)
  They can't forget to take their lunch.
  (= It's important that they remember it.)
- We use *don't have to* when there is no obligation.
  You don't have to give me an answer today. (= You can answer today or another time, it doesn't matter.)
- There is no past form of *must* so we use the past form of *have to* for obligation and no obligation in the past.
  I had to get my hair cut because it was annoying me.
  He had to get a haircut when he joined the army.

Form
- We use the correct form of *must/have to* + the infinitive without *to*.

Common mistakes
- *must* and *have to* have very different meanings in negative sentences.
  don't have to = no obligation
  can't/must not = it's against the rules

should/ought to/had better

Affirmative
I/You/He/She/It/We/They **should see** a doctor.
I/You/He/She/It/We/They **ought to take** a painkiller.
I/You/He/She/It/We/They**'d better put** a bandage on it.

Negative
I/You/He/She/It/We/They **shouldn't go** to bed so late.
I/You/He/She/It/We/They**'d better not dance** with a sprained ankle.

Questions
Should I **put** a bandage on her leg?
Had she **better call** an ambulance?

Short answers
Yes, you **should**. No, you **shouldn't**.
Yes, she **had better**. No, she'd **better not**.

Wh- questions
Where **should** I **put** the cream?
Why **had** they **better see** a doctor?

Adjectives with prepositions

I'm **worried about** that cut on your leg.
She was very **surprised at** winning the gold medal.
Some people are **fascinated by** animals.
Paris is **famous for** the Eiffel Tower.
Is New York very **different from** London?
Living in a city is very exciting.
Are you **frightened of** the dentist?
He's **crazy about** science.
Hong Kong is **similar to** Los Angeles in many ways.
We're all **fed up with** taking tests.
Were they **interested in looking at** your photographs?

should/ought to/had better

Usage
- We use *should(n't)*, *ought to,* and *had better (not)* to give advice, make suggestions, and to say what is right and wrong.
- *should* and *ought* have very similar meanings. However, *should* is much more common than *ought*.
- *had better (not)* means "the best thing to do is . . ." We use *had better (not)* to give slightly stronger advice. It suggests that if you ignore the advice there might be a problem.
  That cut looks serious so you'd better go to the hospital (= If you don't go, you may bleed too much.)

Form
- We use *should(n't)/had better (not)* + the infinitive without *to*.

Common mistakes
You'd better go to bed. ✓
~~You have better go to bed.~~ ✗

Adjectives with prepositions

Usage
- We collocate adjectives with different prepositions:

crazy, sorry, upset, worried	+ about
afraid, frightened, proud, scared, tired	+ of
based	+ on
annoyed, angry, bored, fed up	+ with
different	+ from
famous, responsible, sorry	+ for
bad, good, surprised	+ at
similar	+ to
excited, fascinated	+ by
interested	+ in

Form
- The adjective + preposition is followed by a noun or the gerund (*-ing*) form of a verb.

Grammar Practice

Rules and obligation: *must/have to*

1 ★ **Complete the sentences with the correct form of *must/have to*.**

1 You *don't have to* have an umpire when you play tennis with your friends.

2 My doctor says I _____ do more exercise.

3 I _____ buy any new sneakers this year. These are OK.

4 In the past, Olympic athletes _____ do drugs tests. Now, they are tested frequently to stop cheating.

5 A referee _____ help one of the teams.

6 I'm going for a run in ten minutes but I _____ warm up before I go.

7 You _____ run a marathon if you haven't done any training!

8 I've been playing basketball for an hour. I _____ get a glass of water.

2 ★★ **Complete the text about the rules of chess boxing. Use the verbs in the box with the correct form of *must/have to*.**

> • be • fight • follow • hit • learn • leave
> • not be • play • take off

In chess boxing the two players **1** *have to play* chess and fight each other. The players **2** _____ the normal rules of both sports. They **3** _____ for a few minutes and then they play chess. They have a minute between the two activities to change their clothes. They **4** _____ each other when they are playing chess and obviously, they **5** _____ their gloves to move the chess pieces.

One international champion said, "It's a great sport. You **6** _____ the world's best chess player or boxer but you **7** _____ very good at both sports. However, I **8** _____ to control my anger. Last year, I **9** _____ a tournament because I hit the chess board."

should/ought to/had better

3 ★ **Write advice with *should(n't)/ought to/had better (not)*.**

1 You are getting very heavy.

exercise more / eat so much

You should exercise more. You shouldn't eat so much.

2 Tom twisted his ankle.

sit down / play basketball

_____

_____

3 We're going climbing next weekend.

wear sandals / wear boots

_____

_____

4 I have an insect bite.

put some cream on it / go to the hospital

_____

_____

5 Kate disagrees with the referee.

argue with the referee / accept his decision

_____

_____

6 Leo fell off his bike and cut his leg badly.

ride his bike / clean the cut and put a bandage on it

_____

_____

4 ★★ Write advice. Use the ideas in the box with *should(n't)/ought to/had better (not)*.

- leave before the ambulance arrives
- let him get cold • move him
- move the bicycle • call an ambulance
- ~~put a bandage on her hand~~

1 She should *put a bandage on her hand.*

2 She shouldn't _____

3 She shouldn't _____

4 She ought to _____

5 She'd better _____

6 She'd better not _____

Adjectives with prepositions

5 ★ Complete the sentences with the prepositions from the box.

- about • at • for • ~~of~~ • to • with

1 My little sister is scared *of* dogs.

2 We were all sorry _____ missing the party.

3 I'm annoyed _____ my sister for taking my phone.

4 Mary's phone is similar _____ mine.

5 Who is good _____ English in your class?

6 If you borrow a library book, you are responsible

_____ returning it on time.

6 ★★ Complete the text with the adjectives in the box and the correct prepositions.

- bored • different • famous • interested
- proud • surprised • ~~worried~~

My grandmother flew to Australia last month. At first, she was **1** *worried about* the flight. However, she was **2** _____ how much she enjoyed the journey. She said that the experience was very **3** _____ what she had imagined.

Her visit started in Sydney which is **4** _____ its bridge and opera house. She climbed to the top of the bridge. She was very **5** _____ herself because she has always been frightened of heights.

She took hundreds of pictures of kangaroos and koala bears. I was **6** _____ the first ten pictures but after that I got **7** _____ them!

Consolidation

7 Choose the correct answers.

1 In soccer, the players ___b___ kick each other.
   a) should (b) can't) c) had better not

2 Before you take painkillers, you ____ read the instructions carefully.
   a) mustn't b) have to c) had better not

3 Quick! Greg broke his leg. ____ go to the hospital.
   a) We should b) We must c) We'd better

4 You can get bandages at the supermarket. You __ go to a pharmacy for them.
   a) ought to b) don't have to c) mustn't

5 ____ go swimming if you have a cold. You'll make it worse.
   a) You'd better not b) You ought to
   c) You have to

6 I'm interested ____ learning what to do in an emergency.
   a) at b) in c) of

7 The ambulance driver was ____ for getting the patients to the hospital quickly and safely.
   a) proud b) scared c) responsible